BROADENING HOR

Education and Travelling Children

Sally Naylor and Kanta Wild-Smith

Essex Traveller Education Service

Illustrations by Traveller children in the County of Essex
Additional artwork by Romany Wild-Smith

Essex County Council
Education

Broadening Horizons
Education and Travelling Children

Published by
Essex County Council Education 1997

Price £12.95

ISBN 0904428680

Designed and Produced by Tom Carter and
Sue Copping, Borley Mill, Sudbury, Suffolk.

Printed by R. & K. Tyrrell, Cordell Works,
Cordell Road, Long Melford, Sudbury, Suffolk.

Further copies can be obtained from
Essex County Council Education Department
Information Services
Publications
PO Box 47
Chelmsford CM1 1LD

*Every learner is entitled to benefit from access to a
curriculum and a range of learning experiences of
the highest standard possible, which take account
of unequal starting points and which are provided
irrespective of gender, ethnic background, age or
disability.*

Every Learner – A Framework for the Curriculum in Essex
Essex County Council Education. 1992

CONTENTS

Acknowledgements

We have been grateful for the support, encouragement and
helpful comments of many colleagues. We would like to
thank Jackie Nesbitt, Head of Service and the members of the
Essex Traveller Education Team, particularly Ann Bagehot,
Pat Buck, Sandra Fletcher, Deborah Page, Alan Perkins and
Helen Powell. Thanks also to Mary Waterson, Sue Howell-
Wilson, Mairin Kenny and class teachers and headteachers in
many Essex schools.

We would also like to thank all the Travelling children whose
work is included in this book and the Traveller parents,
whose voice has made an invaluable contribution.

In the course of our work as support teachers with schools and nomadic Traveller children in Essex, we realised that there was a need for some easily accessible background information for schools. The children may be able to stay only a few weeks or months in any one school and the staff may have had no previous contact with Travelling communities. A loose-leaf information pack was compiled based on our experience of the questions and issues commonly raised by school staff.

The pack was found to have a much wider potential audience and this prompted us to include extra material and produce a book. We are not Travellers ourselves and we are aiming only to introduce the reader to some of the issues concerning Travelling children and their education. The book is based on our own experiences and professional knowledge and is not intended to be exhaustive (or exhausting!). There are chapters on the history of the Travelling communities; lifestyles; school life and access to the whole curriculum; the historical context and work of Traveller Education Services; an overview of relevant legislation and a final chapter giving examples of success in improving access, attainment and positive contacts between communities.

This book was stimulated by the needs of a minority within the Traveller population, the most mobile families, who cross both county boundaries and national borders. Travelling children, like all children, have a broad range of experiences and needs. Some live in houses, go to school regularly and are well integrated into their local communities. At the other extreme are the children whose families have no secure stopping place. Although this book focuses on strategies to support children in very difficult educational circumstances, the information is also widely applicable to the work of teachers, trainee teachers and other professionals, with all Travelling children.

Whatever your experience with the Travelling communities we hope you will find something to interest and inspire you in this book.

Sally Naylor and Kanta Wild-Smith
November, 1996

'Entitlement to a full and flexible curriculum' is so central to many current educational debates that the phrase – if not the principle of entitlement itself – is in danger of becoming a cliché. It could become a tired and empty phrase like 'education for all' and 'equality of opportunity' which, in the process of becoming educational and political shorthand, have lost much of their force and impetus. One of the difficulties with articulating matters of principle is that if they are not translated into practice they stay at the level of resounding rhetoric – and do nobody any good.

Whilst debates about education should and must reflect issues of justice and human rights, it is in the everyday practice of education, in the school and classroom environments, that the principles of entitlement are kept alive and are seen to have effects. Teachers themselves can only get to grips with these important matters of equity if they have the chance to translate admirable ideals into what goes on daily with their own classroom communities. But putting principle into practice can be a complex process. Previous practices have to be discarded or unlearned; other people may not share the same views about how best to make ideals into realities; good intentions may lead to bad effects; sometimes ignorance can lead to a new set of prejudices. The materials in this book represent a means of addressing tricky issues of how best to balance the principles and practices of entitlement.

We would want all children to experience tolerance of their home lifestyles and teachers often make strenuous efforts to bridge gaps between home and school. It is often forgotten, however, that the families of the children coming in to school need reassurance that their home values will be respected and valued. This can be a reason for apparent lack of interest in school activities – many adults feel at a disadvantage in relation to school practices and expectations. At the same time, teachers may, for all the best reasons, have mistaken perceptions and assumptions about the home values and experience of the children in their care.

In promoting access to the curriculum, then, there needs to be greater dialogue between the partners in education – the families and teachers whose daily care is for the physical, emotional, social, moral and intellectual development of children. Prejudice is bred from ignorance and an exchange of information is crucial in building confidence and trust. In schools this flow of education has often only been one way – from the school explaining their practices and expectations to families. More recently, attention has been focused on the added benefits to children's education when teachers hear what parents can tell about their children's experience and knowledge. Further to that, it is becoming clear that if teachers can find space within the demands of the curriculum to hear what pupils have to say, then the result is not only greater understanding but a chance to build a more challenging curriculum based on what the learners already know.

Establishing greater common understanding is best done personally, through conversations with families and carers, but this book provides teachers of Travelling children with some informative and helpful starting points. Whilst providing information about Traveller cultural perceptions, it has avoided the danger of generalising. In the same way that it would be impossible fully to summarise the culture of the British house-dwelling population, it is impossible to make generalised assumptions about Travelling families. However, the information provided does give teachers guidance about ways in which fruitful dialogues between home and school might be begun and strengthened.

Much of the curriculum is articulated through reading and writing and literacy holds a critical importance in life generally. In other words, literacy matters. Not having access to literacy matters too, – critically. The legal requirement for all children to attend school means that in the United Kingdom at least, we accept the idea of literacy as an automatic right. Fair enough. But from there it isn't too great a step towards seeing the acquisition of literacy as a kind of duty – either pitying or blaming those individuals in

society who are non-literate or not as fully literate as would be considered acceptable. In this way of course, such individuals or groups receive a double blow; not only do they experience the de-powering effects of not being able to handle the reading and writing demands which others tend to take for granted, but they also suffer from stigma because they lack that power. However, lack of power over the written word is clearly not just a matter of the individual's failure to get the hang of the literacy offered in school. It is first of all to do with access to the school itself. Then, fundamentally, it is dependent on the ways in which literacy opportunities are offered. Unquestioned assumptions about what counts as valid or valuable literacy, can themselves create divisions and exclude some children from ever having the chance to exercise power over their own literacy and so over the social rights which literacy confers.

School should be a place which allows children to extend and strengthen the experiences and knowledge they bring there and use these as a firm basis for future access to the kinds of knowledge and experience which schooling can provide. Shirley Brice Heath *, the American ethnographer, points to the dangers for children's educational futures if there is misunderstanding or misperception between home and school attitudes to children, their language and their learning. Most particularly, she has stressed the impact of differences between literacy and language practices of home and school. Teachers' awareness of the diversity of home language and literacy experience is an essential ingredient in widening the possibilities of future access to learning for all children.

All those involved in education acknowledge the importance of being able to read and write. What is not always so clear or generally agreed, however, is how best to provide the classroom opportunities for pupils to become confidently literate. This book acknowledges the critical importance of literacy to communities who are too often excluded from some of the rights which should be taken for granted in any society wishing to see itself as civilised.

* Shirley Brice Heath (1983) *Ways With Words* Cambridge, Cambridge University Press p.13

Shirley Brice Heath's work also emphasises the importance of spoken forms of language in developing written texts. There is increasing awareness of the important links between language and individual or cultural identity and, crucially, the ways in which these relate to schooled literacy. This means a responsibility on the school and the teacher to be aware of the 'skills, values and knowledge' which the child brings to school. This material acknowledges the importance of valuing Traveller children's language, cultural knowledge and experience. This is particularly important if there is a tendency in the school to confuse the ability to handle abstract concepts with the ability to read and write. It is exactly this kind of unquestioned assumption which excludes pupils from their educational rights. Just because a learner does not have a secure grip on literacy, there is no reason to assume that he or she is 'less able'.

It is becoming increasingly clear that the kinds of texts which are included in any definition of literacy are becoming more varied and diverse, so that it may be necessary to consider a range of *literacies* rather than any one static notion of printed text. As technology advances, there is even more urgency for teachers to review their assumptions about pupils' abilities in handling the literacy demands of the curriculum. Young people now have access to a wide range of texts besides printed books – television, picture books, video, comic books, computer games, interest magazines, CD ROM. The heavy influence of visual and media texts means that attitudes to literacy need to shift, in order to help young readers of new literacies to take a discriminating view of them. Representations need to be viewed and discussed critically.

At the same time, children's knowledge of facts and ideas is being greatly expanded by new forms of presentation. Many of these are part of the social domain and so lend themselves to discussion and argument about their content and meaning and young people are becoming more and more adept at managing the complicated pathways through new technologies. In different ways, then, young learners are coming to take on more powerful roles in respect of the information presented to them outside the classroom.

This offers challenges to teachers to open up class-rooms so that they can hear the voices of the young learners and discover what knowledge, skills and experiences they are bringing to school.

At one and the same time, then, the potential for entitlement to a full and flexible curriculum is threatened and offered hope. On the one hand, there is the danger that narrow and uninformed views will close down opportunities to make schools and classrooms hospitable to diversity. On the other, shifts in technology and educational understanding make that hospitality not only more desirable but increasingly possible. Principle and practice stand between these competing forces. Whilst the requirements of a generalised national curriculum threaten to narrow and restrict classroom possibilities for learning, privileging those who have access to traditional forms of literacy, the impetus of new technologies offers greater opportunities for learning, emphasising the importance of having familiarity with pictorial and oral forms, as well as print.

Besides this, with the development of televisual and telephonic communications, there is greater focus on the spoken word as a means of persuasion, explanation, entertainment and communication. Traditional schooling has favoured the written word and is only now beginning to see the importance of flexible, fluent and confident speakers and listeners. Travelling people, who have found that access to traditional forms of literacy – and so school learning generally – has been a pathway strewn with obstacles, may now find some of those stumbling blocks removed. Until they do, however, there is an urgent need for developing useful dialogues with learners and their families, if entitlement is to be more than an empty phrase. The material in this book makes an important and valuable contribution towards putting principle into practice.

Eve Bearne
Homerton College, Cambridge, October 1996

CHAPTER 1

HISTORICAL PERSPECTIVES

Are They Real Gypsies?

There are a number of different communities who travel in the United Kingdom. There are English and Welsh Romany Gypsies, Irish and Scottish Travellers, Showmen (fairground people) and Circus people. All these communities have a long tradition of a travelling lifestyle, although their history and customs vary. In the second half of this century New Travellers have, for a variety of reasons, adopted a travelling way of life. Some groups travel for long distances around the country, others travel in a closely defined locality.

The term 'Traveller' is generally acceptable to most of these groups. However 'Gypsy' is a term acceptable only to some communities and can be perceived as having negative connotations. The similarity between Romany families and Irish and Scottish Travellers, in occupations and customs, and their equally long tradition of a nomadic lifestyle, make nonsense of the idea that the only true Traveller comes from Romany stock. Fairground people, who prefer to be called 'Showmen', and Circus people, have their own traditional occupations and history of planned movement.

Gypsies and Travellers

Nomadism

> *My granny lived in a tent and all they had to lay on was some straw. They all cuddled up together with one coat over them.*
> *Some of the other Travellers had wagons and some had horse and carts and some had prams to walk up and down with.*
>
> *Ruby, age 10, talking about her family history*

In our highly complicated society, where communities are large and many rights and duties depend, not on face-to-face contact, but on separately held information, it is difficult to prove that you even exist without an address. A nomadic lifestyle fits very uneasily into this sort of society. Travellers find it difficult to fulfil their duties or take advantage of their rights.

People often say "Why don't they settle down?" Perhaps we can gain more insight into this by asking ourselves, "Why don't we take up a nomadic lifestyle?". Where would we begin? How would we earn a living? Where would we go? We have no experience of it. Similarly, Traveller children and their families often have no experience of a settled life. Their perspectives and identities are based on a history of a travelling life.

Approximate numbers of Gypsy/Travellers in Europe

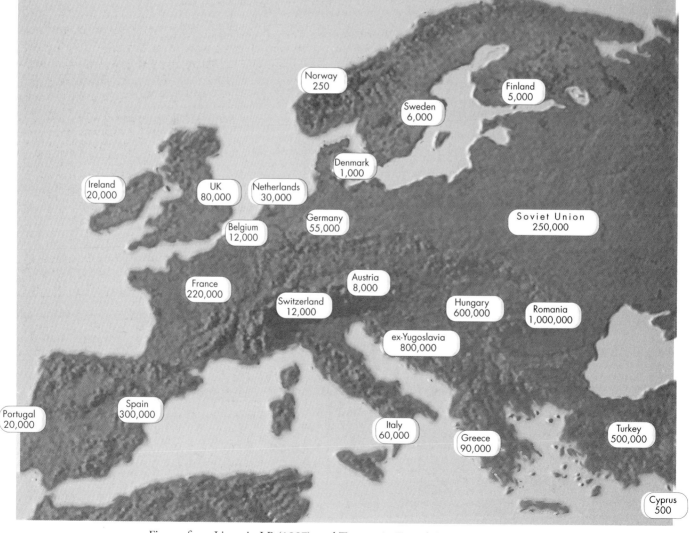

Norway 250
Finland 5,000
Sweden 6,000
Denmark 1,000
Ireland 20,000
UK 80,000
Netherlands 30,000
Soviet Union 250,000
Germany 55,000
Belgium 12,000
France 220,000
Austria 8,000
Switzerland 12,000
Hungary 600,000
Romania 1,000,000
ex-Yugoslavia 800,000
Spain 300,000
Portugal 20,000
Italy 60,000
Greece 90,000
Turkey 500,000
Cyprus 500

Figures from Liegeois, J.P. (1987), and Tomasevic, B. and Djuric, P. (1989), quoted in O'Reilly, M. (1993)

Economic History

Evidence indicates that Gypsy people first migrated into Europe from India in the Middle Ages and arrived in this country in the 15th century. It was thought at the time that they had come from Egypt, hence the word Gypsy from 'Egyptian'. Indigenous Travelling people already existed in most of Europe. In the British Isles they worked at such trades as mending and selling pots and pans, knife and tool grinding, hawking and trading in a variety of goods, including home-made artefacts and horses, as well as providing seasonal agricultural labour and entertainment. In rural areas Gypsies and Travellers also had an important role as bringers of news and information.

In *The Education of Gypsy and Traveller Children, Action Research and Co-ordination* (ACERT edit. 1993), Nathan Lee estimates that the largest group in the United Kingdom are the Romanichals (around 61,000, about half of whom may be classed as nomadic, or, when living on authorised sites, semi-nomadic). These figures do not take account of the many Gypsy families who have settled into housing, some for several generations. In the last few decades seasonal agricultural work has become virtually non-existent due to increasing mechanisation. The rural Gypsy parents of the present school population would have returned annually to the same farms, working at, for example, fruit picking in Kent, strawberry picking in Cambridgeshire, hoeing vegetables in winter and potato picking in autumn. Their grandparents would have travelled continuously from farm to farm throughout the year. In the last few decades seasonal agricultural work has become virtually non-existent due to increasing mechanisation.

Other Travelling groups in the United Kingdom are the Scottish Travellers (around 19,000 people, about two-thirds estimated to be sedentary), the Irish Travellers (around 15,000 with about two-thirds being sedentary, although this is an estimate and changes constantly) and the Welsh Travellers (numbering about 2,000, the majority of whom are believed to be sedentary). The Irish Travellers seem to be the most highly mobile group and in recent years, the most urban. Whilst members of all groups would have depended to some extent on seasonal agricultural work, Irish Travellers were known for their work with metals, especially tin. Since the mid-1980s another important occupation, the collecting and selling of scrap metal for recycling, has also provided much less revenue.

The population of Travellers and Gypsies in any individual country is difficult to determine for many reasons. However O'Reilly (1993) suggests that there are 12 to 15 million Travellers worldwide of which

Tracey, age 13

three to five million live in Europe. He cites the figures on the map *(see page 6)* as conservative estimates of the European national populations.

These European groups often have no solid links with one another. The strongest common feature may be that they speak different dialects of one, possibly two, ancient Indian languages. These were spoken by nomadic groups who left India about 1,000 years ago. They also share elements of a common culture, most importantly, a great emphasis on cleanliness as an organising principle.

Today, the economy of the highly mobile groups in the United Kingdom includes trading in carpets, furniture, antiques, laying tarmac, roofing, tree felling and pruning, landscape gardening and road building. Increasingly, families are travelling to other European countries to find work, especially Germany. The main characteristics of the Traveller and Gypsy economy for both rural and urban mobile groups, has always been flexibility and adaptability. Mobile families stay largely outside the system of waged labour, except as one element in a range of activities. Of course, Travellers and Gypsies with a more settled lifestyle may, and do, take up any of the occupations open to the settled community. Many do not publicly acknowledge their Gypsy/Traveller background because of the adverse effects of prejudiced attitudes and stereotypes.

Language, Dialect and Accent

Anglo-Romani (poggerdi jib, literally 'broken tongue') is the name given to a dialect of English, spoken by Romany Gypsies, which has been handed down orally over the generations. Romani speech was first recorded in 1542 and has gradually become more anglicised. Nowadays Romani words are still used and additional words have been borrowed from other sources such as regional dialects, slang, Cant and older forms of English. Knowledge and use of Anglo-Romani varies from family to family and the words in common use vary between regions. Many families consider that the language should be kept secret.

There are secret languages associated with Irish and Scottish Traveller communities called Cant and Gammon and Shelta. The languages appear, in part, to be formed by adapting Gaelic words. Irish Traveller children often speak with strong Irish accents, though they may never have been to Ireland. Anglo-Irish can be quite distinctive in its sentence construction, for example, "That there fella's been

boxin' me" (That boy over there has been hitting me). English Gypsy speech also has its own distinctive structures and vocabulary with, at present, little influence from written English. Many Gypsies regularise irregular verbs or use alternatives, for example, run-runned, catch-cotched, give-gov.

Some words, commonly heard in Essex, are listed below, together with their origins.

Ind = related to Sanskrit, linking the geographical origin of the Romany Gypsies to India. *

kushti (Ind)	nice, lovely
mokkadi (Roumanian)	unclean
dinilo (Ind)	crazy, mad
divvi (Slav)	stupid, silly
chavvi (Ind)	boy, son
frit (slang)	frightened
mort (Scots Cant)	woman
mush (Ind)	man
chai (Ind)	daughter, girl
rakkli (Ind)	woman
trailer	caravan
gaugo (pronounced gorja)	non-Gypsy
ladged (Ind)	embarrassed
dik akai (Ind)	look here
holler	shout
bold, brazen	impolite

Some families consider it unlucky to say certain words aloud, monkey and rat being the most common. When these words come up in reading schemes, with characters like Bangers and Mash and Deb the Rat, children may prefer to substitute gorilla or chimpanzee and 'long-tail'.

*See Acton T. and Kendrick D. (1984) *Rokkeripen To-Divvus* Romanistan Publications, London

Local History

What knowledge do you already have about Gypsies and Travellers in your locality? Below are a few questions to discuss with colleagues.

1 Do Gypsies and Travellers visit this area?

2 Do they stay in the same areas of the town or countryside?

3 Are there memories of Gypsy or Traveller families from among older residents?

4 Is there any written evidence of Gypsy or Traveller families, for example local histories, gravestones, road names?

5 Do you know any surnames which are Gypsy or Traveller names? Would you be able to identify a Gypsy or Traveller standing next to you in a queue in the supermarket? How?

6 What sort of work did Gypsies and Travellers do in this area? What sort of work do they do now?

7 Do you know any Gypsies or Travellers personally, or know anyone who knows a family?

8 What sort of links do you think families have with the different areas in which they spend their time?

9 Consider these statements, which are contemporary views about Travellers.* Which do you agree or disagree with? Would your view affect your professional interaction with Travellers?

  a) Travellers are the same as everybody else.
  b) Travellers are social misfits and deviants.
  c) Travellers are a subculture of poverty.
  d) Travellers are colourful and exotic nomads.
  e) Travellers are an ethnic, nomadic group.

---

* Statements a) to e) by John O'Connell, Director, Dublin Travellers Education and Development Group, in M. Kenny and M. O'Reilly (1995) *Blackstones round the Green Shamrock* Pavee Point, Dublin

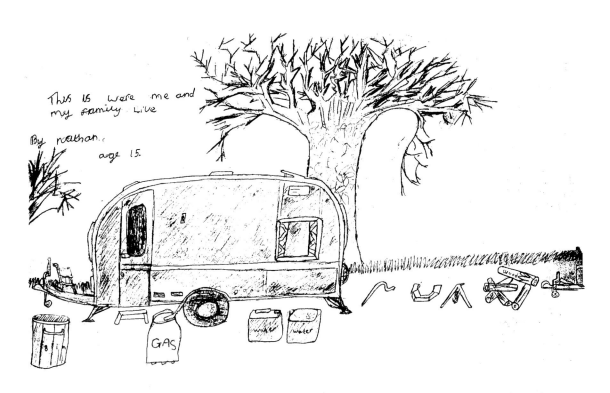

This is were me and my family live

By nathan. age 15.

GAS

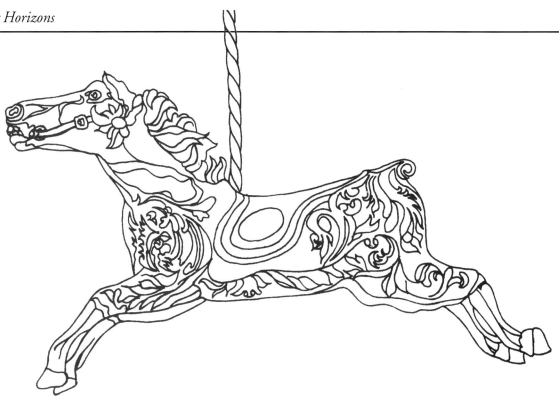

Showmen and Circus People

Fairgrounds

The word 'fair' is derived from the Latin word 'feria' meaning holiday, but it is thought that the origins of the fair go back past the Roman occupation of Britain to the seasonal gatherings held in prehistoric times. The two important elements of trade and festivity have continued down the ages. An example of an ancient fair which survived into this century is Weyhill Fair in Hampshire, which was held on an isolated hill top at the meeting point of two important prehistoric trade routes, the Gold Road from Wales and the Tin Road from Cornwall.

In the Middle Ages charters granted by the sovereign gave the fair legal status and increasing economic importance. Merchants from Europe brought goods to trade from all over the world: Italian silks, Spanish iron, French wine and precious stones and spices from the East via Moscow. No fewer than 4,860 fairs were chartered between 1200 and 1400. The fairs drew not only merchants but travelling entertainers as well: jugglers, musicians and tumblers – the ancestors of today's Showmen.

The Black Death of 1348-9 brought a new kind of fair. In order to stem the rise in wages caused by the shortage of agricultural labourers, Edward III introduced the Statute of Labourers. This compelled all able-bodied men to present themselves annually for hire at a stated wage. These hiring fairs, or mop fairs,

were held mainly around Michaelmas, the end of the agricultural year, and continued until as late as the 1920s in some rural areas.

By the early 18th century the trading aspect of the charter fairs had waned and fairs consisted almost entirely of amusements. There were travelling theatre companies with traditions of news bringing, political satire and melodrama, puppet plays, slightly risqué shows like striptease, peepshows; anything that was strange, novel or bizarre, like the bearded woman, contortionists and illusionists.

Also at around this time the first fairground rides appeared. An engraving of 1808, of Bartholomew Fair held on London's Smithfield, shows early wooden rides propelled by gangs of boys. The rides look small and insignificant in the background beside the substantial, brightly lit booths and side-shows.

In 1868 the first steam driven roundabout was invented. Freed from the limitations imposed by muscle power, fairground rides became more and more inventive in their design and more elaborately carved and decorated. The Victorian Fair was epitomised by the beautiful Galloping Horses and the sound of mechanical organ music. Other innovations were often first seen by country people at fairs, including electric lighting and moving pictures, but it was the rides which were the most important attraction by the time of the First World War and have remained so to this day.

The Circus

It is thought that Philip Astley staged the first modern circus in London in 1768. He was a sergeant major in the English cavalry and performed as a trick rider. He introduced circuses in cities throughout Europe. By the beginning of the 19th century there were permanent circuses in many large continental European cities as well as small travelling shows which used caravans of covered wagons to transport and accommodate performers and equipment.

The travelling shows would originally have consisted of a musician, jugglers and acrobats, performing in open spaces and taking a collection. This developed into performances in enclosed spaces where admission was charged. No one is certain whether tents were introduced first in Europe or the United States but they were probably not used until about 1820.

Elaborate equestrian performances were common features of early permanent circuses. Rope-dancing, juggling, acrobatic, wild-animal and clowning acts were all incorporated as the circus developed as an entertainment throughout the United States and Europe in the 19th century. Later additions to the repertoire were the flying trapeze, which was invented in 1859, and the street parade and side-show.

The multi-ring circus was a phenomenon peculiar to the United States. Barnum and Bailey's circus was so huge that it was staged simultaneously in three rings. The Circus Corporation of America, formed in 1929 by Barnum and Bailey and the Ringling Brothers was, at the height of its popularity, the largest touring organisation in the world, using 300 tents to stage a show and carrying its own diesel plants to generate electricity.

New Travellers

Our experience in Essex of working with New Traveller families is limited. In their case, an historical perspective is relatively very short and their history and culture are in the making. In recent years many children have been born into these communities and know no other lifestyle.

There are a multitude of reasons why people adopted a nomadic lifestyle. Negative reasons, that is needing to get away from something, included homelessness, or very poor standards of accommodation and painful personal situations. Positive choices to travel were often made on ecological, environmental and political grounds.

"Other positive reasons include the reaction against the constant consumerism of Society today. The clutter of possessions and their supposed value can be left behind. The importance of money reduces and other qualities become more relevant... People need much less space and some Travellers believe that a nomadic existence is that which the planet can sustain most successfully. Reflecting that, another reason is to be closer to the earth and nature... A Traveller has to take note of surroundings, and some do their best to live in harmony with the earth." *

---

* Fiona Earle, Alan Dearling, Helen Whittle, Roddy Glasse and Gubby, 1994. *A Time to Travel*, pp 50–51

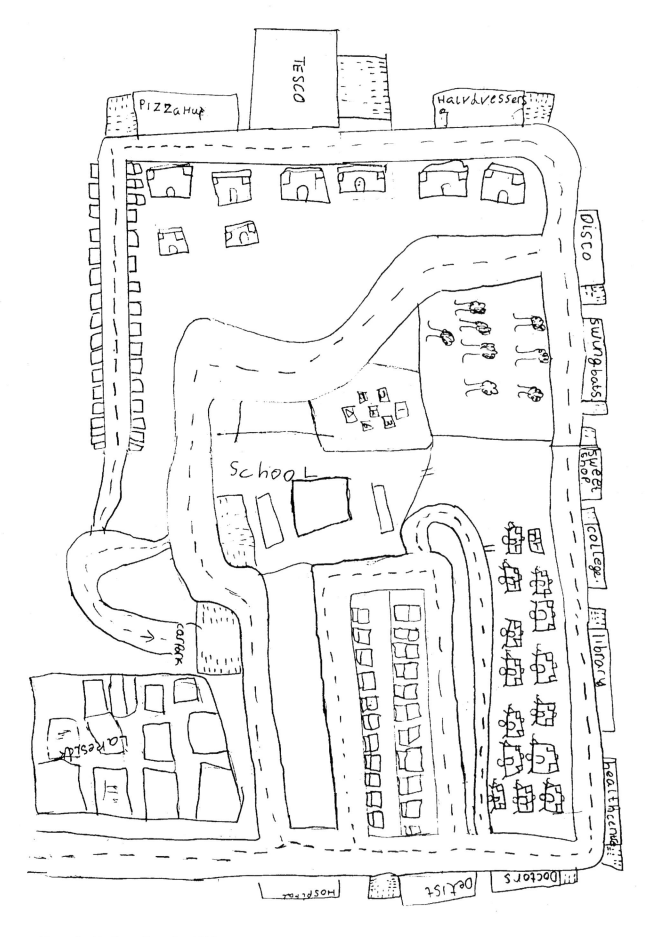

Ann, age 10, at school in Essex, December 1996

CHAPTER 2

LIFESTYLES

This chapter describes elements of the lifestyle of continuously mobile families with no legal stopping place. Many of the elements described apply equally to more settled Traveller families, for whom mobility remains an important part of their cultural identity. Also included is a section on living at the fair and circus. The economic lifestyle of many of these families has a pattern of seasonal travelling. For education purposes the children from all these communities may be supported by the network of Traveller Education Services nationally.

"I'll never stop travelling really. I mean it's just like getting a bird now, getting a real wild thing, putting them in a cage, they'll die. I like travelling but not in the frosty winter, I like settling… In the summer time, I like travelling. It's like a person born coloured black. You can't change the colour of their skin. We're Travellers and that's our life. We're used to that sort of world. That's all we're used to. That's what they're even saying in Parliament. We're Travelling people, we're here and that's it."

An Irish Traveller woman talking about travelling
October 1996

Gypsies and Travellers

Lifestyle on the Roadside

Living on the roadside and moving from place to place means that families are vulnerable in a number of ways. The ground around the trailer does not belong to them. Anyone can walk on it. Anyone can knock on the bedroom door in the middle of the night. Activities outside the trailer are immediately visible to passers-by and it is difficult for individual families to control the space around their trailer. Travellers also gain a very strong impression from government legislation, the police, television reporting and members of the local community that they are not wanted, so there is little incentive to be community spirited themselves.

Travellers often have no sense of belonging to a geographical place. On meeting someone for the first time, you might ask where they come from and this would be a significant part of their personal history. For Travellers there is often no geographical element to their personal identity.

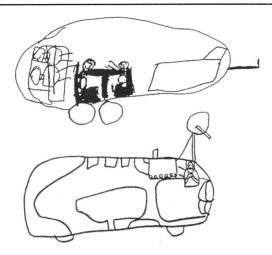

Cross-section of their trailer drawn by Johnny and Tommy, ages 10 and 8, at school in Essex April to June 1995

Community belonging is based on extended family ties. A mother, newly moved into a house, might ask a neighbour about local schools. A Traveller mother, who has brought her community with her, has limited means of finding out what is available in different geographically located communities. Information, support and reassurance about schooling are difficult to come by, especially if you are not literate or some elements of the settled community are overtly hostile. Adults within the extended family group tend to be very warm and caring towards the children and sometimes seem quite over-protective.

However, this protectiveness can be understood in light of the level of hostile incidents encountered.

"I walked back to the camp after school with the children, to speak to their parents. I was talking to two of the children and three had run ahead of us. On the corner, before they turned into the camp site, I became aware of a group of boys, from the school, waiting. They raised their arms, as if to throw something, but then noticed that I was just behind. I guess they had seen me in school, because they dropped the stones they had been holding, onto the ground, and ran off across the field."

Traveller Education Service Support Teacher

Groups of families living on the roadside do not stay together all the time. They are forming and re-forming quite frequently for all sorts of different reasons: to support a sister who is having a new baby; a mother who is ill; a brother who has some work in Germany. With quite large families, the number of different combinations of brothers, sisters and connections by marriage is considerable. It is not uncommon for children of all ages to stay with relations for long periods of time.

What looks like a community from the outside may be two or more quite unrelated family groups, who may not necessarily know each other. One grandmother described how another unrelated Traveller family tipped hard-core right outside her bedroom window and she could do nothing about it. Conversely, what looks like a group from the outside might be just one family with two or more trailers. Sometimes there is a 'best' trailer, a cooking trailer and a trailer for older children.

Water collection and storage has to be carefully organised by a Traveller family. Imagine how your life at home would change without clean, running water on tap. Children in school are often very appreciative of hot running water and flushing toilets. They may need to be shown how to use them and are often very interested in where the piped water comes from and where it goes to. Some children may be reluctant to use the toilets if the pipes hiss and the tank gurgles. Plumbing may need to be explained and fears taken seriously.

This is my Dad going to get water.

He goes to my uncel's House to get water. By NATHAN

Inside space for everything is very limited. This affects shopping for food, cooking, clothes and laundry, play, toys, hobbies, sleeping habits, personal privacy, evening activities, in fact, every aspect of life. Storage for anything that is not being used regularly is non-existent and it is virtually impossible to keep anything out of reach of younger brothers or sisters. The weather also has an important effect on family activities, as anyone who has been on holiday in a caravan without an awning will appreciate.

Self-employment means that family routines can be quite individual. The very time-regulated routines of the school day are quite different. Many activities in the home, such as the daily shopping, collecting water, cleaning, polishing and tidying the trailer, going for a shower at a swimming pool or leisure centre and feeding the family, need not be regulated by the clock.

GOING FOR TAR

The hard core yard.

We got up in the morning and we got the tools ready. Daddy built up air in the lorry. We went to the hard-core yard. The man filled up the lorry with hard-core on his JCB. Then we went to our job.

going to the job

Tipping up the hard core

The day before we already dug it out. Then we put the hard-core in the drive. Then he got the backer plate and hit it down. He measured with a tape measure to see if it was deep enough for the tar. Then we went for the tar to the tar yard.

UNDER THE TAR CHUTE

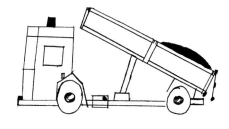

At the tar yard the man said "We only have three ton left." We wanted three and a half ton of red tar. We waited for half an hour to get it properly mixed. The man said "Right it's ready." We reversed the lorry in under the tar chute.

   Then we covered the tar up with two or three tar covers. We drove back to the job. We laid down the tar and my dad rolled it with a vibrator. We put in the chippings at the same time as we are rolling. Then it looks really good. It takes about two or three days to complete a tarmac job, one day for digging out and one or two days for hard-core and tarmacking.

Simon   age 12

Children are absorbed into the family economic structure at a much younger age than is usual in today's settled population. Boys are expected to be working with their fathers by the age of 11 or 12 Girls of that age take responsibility for cleaning tasks and the care of younger siblings, sometimes while their mother is out working or shopping. By the roadside, the trailer is rarely left without a family member to watch it. In general, roles within the family are based on traditional ideas about gender.

The importance of this traditional pattern of family employment was underlined by a Traveller mother, who was explaining her opposition to the enrolment of her son at secondary school, though his older sister had taken GCSE examinations.

" Well… he's got to learn to be a Traveller, when else will he do it? What use will a GCSE be to him? I didn't mind her going but if they try to make me send him, we'll go back on the road."

Mother, with place on an authorised site, summer travelling

Children's Names

Children's names may differ from those in common use in the settled community. In all Gypsy and Traveller groups traditional names are in frequent use, often being associated with a grandparent or other important family member.

A feature of Irish Traveller groups, in particular, is their use of maternal and paternal surnames interchangeably. This can be confusing to those outside the community, especially as children may also have a baptismal first name and a 'family' name. It is traditional to name first sons and daughters after their grandparents. In a large family group there may be, for example, three or four cousins with the same names. Thus the need for family names can be appreciated. Below are some examples of first names, less common in the settled community but used relatively frequently in Travelling families.

Philomena	Jeremiah
Dorcas (Darkie)	Seana or Shuna
Prissella	Shadrack (Shady)
Levi	Eli
Angelina	Hughie
Maryann	Miles (Miley)

Dates of Birth

Dates of birth and birth certificates are not given as much significance in most Travelling families as they are in the literate, settled community. Whilst most families are aware that the majority of schools group children according to chronological age, they will often request education in family groups. This is, in

the families' view, preferable and in sympathy with the home tradition.

The community is not dominated by routines associated with time. Days of the week and months of the year do not always have a great deal of significance. Children will often say they are 'eight', meaning 'in their eighth year'. They may, in fact, just have had their seventh birthday. Mothers may sometimes be unsure of their child's date of birth or offer an inaccurate age, because of a genuine wish to educate their child alongside particular cousins of that age. Care in explaining the organisation of a school, and times when family members will be able to meet, can help in allaying fears.

Religious Affiliation

Religious affiliation often has enormous significance in the life of Traveller families. Irish Travellers are most often practising Roman Catholics and will sometimes request a Roman Catholic school for their children. In recent times, the evangelical Gypsy church has become very significant in the lives of many English Gypsy Travellers. Families may travel quite long distances to church meetings.

As in some settled families, weddings and funerals are the occasion for large family gatherings, with much ceremonial attached. Other events of importance in the religious calendar or of particular personal significance, such as First Communion and grave praying, may also be reasons for an extended family gathering. Large groups of trailers may gather by the roadside, in advance of such an occasion.

Writing by Mark, age 12, at secondary school in Essex 1994/95

Drawing and writing by John, age 8. 'Appleby Horse Fair'

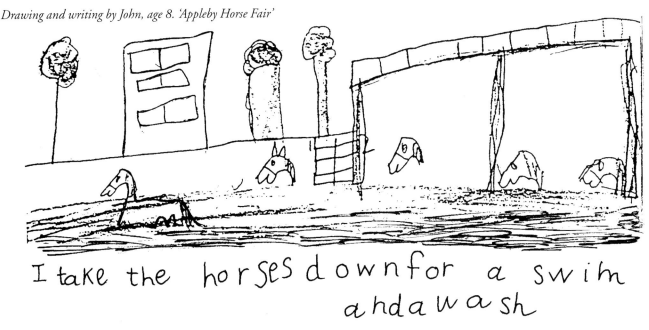

I take the horses down for a swim and a wash

Traditional Fairs

Fairs have traditionally been important meeting places for Travellers. Appleby Horse Fair in Westmorland is one very large traditional fair which takes place in June each year. As well as buying and selling horses and domestic goods, Travellers come to meet their friends and family in a holiday atmosphere. Stow Fair in Gloucestershire, Cambridge Fair and Epsom Races have also been important annual venues.

Fairground and Circus Life

Travelling Fairs

The men, women and children who live and work at travelling fairs are known as Showmen. Their lifestyle varies considerably according to the season. About half the year is spent travelling with the fair and the rest of the time is spent at home in winter quarters.

Joe, age 9, at school in Essex

Living at the Fair

The season starts around Easter time. Travelling fairs move every one to two weeks, usually packing up on Sunday and Monday, travelling part of Monday and Tuesday and setting up again ready to open to the public on Wednesday night. Families sometimes live in touring caravans, but more often in very large caravans (trailers) which are more like mobile homes on wheels, with two or three spacious rooms. A substantial stairway with a covered canvas porch leads to the door, which is about three feet off the ground. Smaller tourers are often used by teenage family members as independent living accommodation.

The fair opens to the public at about five or six o'clock. Children often have close contact with the details of their parents work from an early age. Fairs close at around eleven o'clock and clearing up and securing the rides, booths and stalls may take another hour. Children normally go to bed before their parents but don't always get up before them in the morning.

The fair boss, the lessee, rents the fairground location and is responsible for the smooth running of the fair in accordance with the rules of the Showmen's Guild. All owners of travelling fairground rides and booths must be members of the Guild and the rules cover safety, environmental health and facilities for the families while living on a fairground and also in winter quarters.

A fair does not move as one entity to each new location. Some families follow a similar pattern year after year on an established route, others are trying to fill their season and gain a regular routine. Many Essex families travel almost exclusively within Essex during the season. Others travel widely throughout the

country and are not seen from the beginning of the season until the time they pull back in for the winter. Likewise families who winter in other counties come to work at fairs in Essex in the summer.

Living in Winter Quarters

When the travelling season has finished, usually some time in October, families pull back to the yard. The rides, booths and stalls are repaired, repainted and stored. Some parents are taking winter jobs to tide them over until the spring. The winter season is also a time for annual holidays, weddings and other celebrations. Approximately 150 Showmen families reside in Essex each winter.

The Circus

Circus families also have a seasonal pattern to their lives. Circus proprietors are regulated by the Showmen's Guild in respect of animal health and welfare and the environmental health, safety, rights and obligations of families while travelling and in winter quarters.

Children who travel with a circus may be performers themselves or the children of performing artists. Circuses are more likely than travelling fairs to cross national boundaries or possibly to winter in a country other than the United Kingdom. Performers in the circus may come from many different countries and their first language may not be English. Each season circuses of varying sizes travel in the United Kingdom.

by Fred

CHAPTER 3

SCHOOL LIFE

School staff may assume a certain knowledge of the conventions and language associated with school life. This chapter alerts staff to areas where children and parents may need additional support or explanation.

Traveller parents may have had little or no experience of school themselves, have little contact with the local community and generally feel that they are not wanted wherever they go. Confidence and trust between schools and Travellers needs to be built up so that Travelling children can feel safe enough to come to school and secure and valued enough to benefit from the multitude of what may be strange, new learning experiences.

Traveller Education Support Services can facilitate a mutual exchange of information between school and parents about expectations and routines. This is particularly useful where parents are not literate. There is a great deal of detail to be absorbed and this is difficult when written checklists and booklets cannot be used for reference.

Exploring a New Environment

School life is so different from life on the roadside that the experience can be usefully compared to travelling in a foreign country, where the language, customs, rules and regulations are all unknown. It can be very confusing and worrying. The children have to travel on their own, and when parents have little knowledge of school they find it difficult to help their children, or get a clear picture of what is actually happening in school. Many of the children are very enthusiastic about school and, like their parents, place great emphasis on learning to read and write. At first the need for a broader curriculum may not always be appreciated.

Patience and understanding will help the children considerably, particularly in the following broad areas.

School Language

What could these mean?
  assembly
  break
  tuck
  colour it in
  turn over (heard when sharing a book,
      not in Physical Education)
  wipe your feet
  look up (in a book)
  get in line

Even fundamental ideas such as what constitutes a 'class' may not be obvious, particularly in an open-plan school.

Reception class teachers are used to teaching new vocabulary and checking for understanding, but it is easy to assume, unconsciously, that children of a certain age will have had a certain amount of schooling.

Although children pick up a great deal by copying others, time given to checking for understanding is very reassuring to a child in a strange situation. This can avoid children feeling stupid or naughty.

Social Customs and School Rules

Travelling children often address adults very directly, with little concern for relationship or status. Accepted forms of address may need to be taught and gradually learned. For instance:

* how to attract the teacher's attention;
* how to answer the register;
* how to show that you are ready to answer a question.

Some children pick these things up effortlessly but others benefit from explicit teaching.

Social customs change from school to school and may need to be re-learned. Examples of such customs and routines might be:

* dining hall routines,
* when it is necessary to ask a teacher's permission,
* which doors can be used,
* playground rules and boundaries,
* when talking is allowed,
* what sort of 'tuck' is allowed.

The details of these routines and social habits can be difficult to remember at first, as anyone who has changed jobs recently will remember, and as peripatetic teachers experience daily. Travelling children may have attended a number of different schools for a short time, be returning to school after a long period away, or be starting school for the first time in the junior or secondary phase. Sometimes there seems to be no obvious reason why some behaviours are

required, rather than others, or why everyone has to behave in the same way. Explanations are always helpful. It takes time before all the details can be absorbed.

The older you are, the more people assume that you know things and the more uncomfortable it is to be ignorant of the customs.

"The importance of the individual in the community is recognised when we:

...try to ensure that the rules and rituals which govern daily life are understood, shared and supported by the community within the establishment and the community it serves.
...are sensitive also to rules and rituals which are followed by individuals, even if they are different from those widely accepted by the local community. A positive effort is made to discover and understand what beliefs and values are held by the members of the community and to find ways of exploring their contribution to the well-being of the community as a whole."

Every Learner – A Framework for the Curriculum in Essex

Exploration and Discovery

Travelling children are used to living in caravans, where space is very limited, there are no stairs and furniture is built in. The experience of being in a building, let alone such a large one as a school, with such a variety of uses of space and furniture, differs greatly from home. The discipline style, accent and vocabulary of the teachers and other staff can also be different from the adults at home.

Opportunities for play with construction toys, board games, paint, water and sometimes pens, pencils and paper are extremely limited or non-existent in the small space and limited storage provided by a caravan. Time to explore the large, warm and dry, open space, time to investigate drawers and cupboards and time to experience running water may all be necessary for Traveller children to become familiar with their new environment. This is especially important when they have missed all, or part of, the vital Reception year.

Time, used as a restraint, is foreign to many Traveller pupils. To them, time is usually much more flexible around a task in hand. The perplexing custom of packing away when not finished and putting models or jigsaws away when not complete, needs careful treatment to avoid upset and conflict.

There is no doubt that children need time to investigate and explore. Similarly, children need to be able to use toys, equipment and materials in an unstructured way, before they can successfully use them for more focused tasks. Legitimate time allowed for exploration, perhaps with the help of another pupil, allows the child to conform to realistic expectations, rather than being seen, or seeing herself, as 'off-task'. As one reception teacher, with a class who had been in school for one term, talking about a Traveller child new to school, so simply put it,

"I just need to give her time to experience what everyone else takes for granted."

At first, this may seem impossible to organise, especially for older children. However, more practical activities could prove beneficial for some other children in the class. Helping to organise practical tasks, or a tour of where equipment is kept, could be an invaluable boost to the confidence of children, who are usually on the receiving end of help themselves.

Midday and Playground Assistants

Midday and Playground Assistants may find it useful to bear in mind the following information, which has often been significant in our experience. It is by no means exclusive to children from Traveller families.

• **Grouping together** in the playground may look like threatening, almost 'gang-like' behaviour but is much more likely to be for reassurance and support in a strange new place.

- **Older children** may wish, or have been told by families, to look after younger siblings. This can cause difficulties if infants and juniors are normally in separate playgrounds. Family relationships are very close and protective.

- **On the roadside**, children will have been used to exploring, digging, climbing and examining anything they find, in an often hazardous environment. They will spend their time outside, in mixed age groups, older children 'minding' younger family members. A concrete playground, without very obvious restrictions on what can be touched or climbed on and with an emphasis on social games can be a new experience. Play can tend to be more boisterous than some children are used to.

- **The smallest incident of name-calling** needs to be challenged. Children may expect hostility from adults as well as other children and probably will not report such incidents, unless actively encouraged to do so. Sensitively managed, this can make the whole school experience a positive one.

- **Very young children** may not understand that they have easy access to a toilet and running water to wash their hands. Alternatively, if access is restricted, they need to understand, in advance, what the restrictions are. Children may need some explanation of the arrangements for flushing the toilet and to be reassured that gurgling and rushing noises from the pipes are quite usual and nothing to be frightened about.

- **Some children will know what is acceptable language** in school and others will not. If possible, a quiet explanation would be preferable to a public condemnation.

- **Space in a trailer** is very restricted and, occasionally, children may have had limited experience of eating at a table with a knife and fork. Food can tend to be eaten on knees using spoons or fingers.

The playground, where everything is more fluid and uncertain than the classroom, can be the most important place to ensure that school is a happy and successful experience.

One headteacher remembers an incident which illuminated for her the existence of a separate but equally valid set of values.

She was crossing from the junior building to the infant building during lesson time, when she observed Ben, a newly arrived reception child, quietly walking towards the end of the field. He stopped by some trees but it was difficult to see exactly what he was doing. She waited to see how things would develop but almost immediately he came back again. He became aware of her and she called out "Are you alright, Ben?" He waved and said, in a matter of fact voice "It's alright Miss, I've just been to be sick." She put her arm around him and they walked together back into the classroom.

A child was talking to his teacher as one independent person to another, at ease with himself and wanting to reassure someone who was concerned about him.

School Secretaries and Receptionists

A welcoming face on entering a school is especially important. Parents need to feel sure that their children will be safe and happy before entrusting them to 'strangers'. Children may have to face entering new schools 12 to 15 times a year if the families move on frequently.

School secretaries and receptionists will often be the first people in a school with whom parents have contact. The following information may be useful as a guide to some of the less familiar administrative work necessary at the time of admission of Traveller pupils and to aid understanding of the perspective of Traveller parents.

Traveller parents vary considerably in the amount of experience they have had of school. Some parents will never have been inside a school building. Some may have had only brief periods in school. There may

have been upsetting experiences of name-calling or physical bullying while in school. Additionally some parents may feel embarrassed by their inability to read and write.

Added to these uneasy feelings about schooling may be a general background of hostility and rejection by the local settled population, felt by mobile and other Travellers in their everyday lives. School staff may also feel uneasy about how best to help people who come from a cultural background they know little about and who may only be staying for a short time.

Some important points about admission procedures for nomadic Travellers.
- There may be no emergency contact number as few families have mobile phones. Parents may say that anyone on the site would take responsibility for their children in an emergency.
- The family may not be registered with a doctor.
- Some parents may not feel able to read the form or to write the information on to the form themselves. Occasionally they may be unable to sign their name and need to make a mark.
- 'Green Cards' may be offered by parents. These are Department for Education and Employment (DfEE) Record Reference Cards which have been produced to facilitate the transfer of records between schools. They are retained by parents and need to be stamped and dated by each admitting school. *

Essex records the admission and departure of Traveller children on a special form, in order to collect accurate information for the DfEE. Other areas will have their own procedures.

It will be especially important to retain patience and good humour when faced with parents who have a limited experience of school language, behaviour and routines. Some parents may have been asked for information they are unable to provide in a number of different schools and may be prepared for rejection. Understanding their perspective will help smooth the process for everyone involved.

Attendance

The special position of Traveller children is recognised by section 199 of the Education Act 1993 which protects Traveller parents from conviction if they are engaged in trade or business which requires travelling from place to place. This does not mean that part-time education for Traveller children is legally acceptable. The aim should be to attend school as regularly as possible but a balance has to be struck between, on the one hand, the need for action in individual cases in the interests of the child, and on the other, adopting a sensitive and sympathetic approach which recognises the lifestyle and cultural tradition of the family concerned. The child should attend a school as a registered pupil as regularly as the trade permits and, after the age of six, should make at least 200 attendances during the preceding twelve months. Parents should ensure that children are receiving suitable education when not at school.

Attendance Registers

Schools may authorise the absence of Traveller children if they are satisfied that the family is travelling, but has indicated that there is an intention to return.

"Some schools in these circumstances are able to maintain contact with the children by outreach work or distance learning packs, although such activities should not be viewed as a preferable alternative to attendance at school. Some reasonable latitude on absence might also be offered in respect of families who have moved from, or have been evicted from, unauthorised sites while the family finds another site… all efforts should be made to encourage maintenance of attendance at school." **

---

*see also section on Names and Dates of Birth
** *School Attendance. Policy and Practice on Categorisation of Absence.* DfEE 1994

Education Welfare Officers

Some authorities also employ specialist education welfare officers, field officers or home-school liaison workers, who are familiar with the cultural background of Traveller families. Working practices will vary between authorities, but the aim will always be to secure and maintain the children's attendance at school.

Home to School Transport

Travelling children may qualify for transport to school in the same way as all children, under a county's particular rules about entitlement. Many parents can and do transport their own children to school. However there are also genuine cases of need where exceptional transport is a crucial factor in securing the children's attendance at school, both initially and on a day-to-day basis. Many mothers are still left in isolated situations without transportation when husbands need vehicles for work and some families are particularly wary of walking to school in a neighbourhood which they perceive, often correctly, to be hostile. Additionally, where there is a large unauthorised encampment the local school is not usually expected to take all of the children. Families may be forced to undertake longer journeys to school than most settled people would choose.

In recognition of the particular problems which some Traveller families face, Traveller Education Services are sometimes able to assist with home to school transport from their own budgets, at the discretion of the Head of Service. Services who have this facility may organise it in different ways according to the local situation.

Particular Issues concerning Secondary Education

Access and Transfer

"Access to the curriculum for secondary aged children remains a matter of grave concern. There are as many as 10,000 children at this phase who are not even registered with a school." *

The transfer to secondary education at 11 is a big change for all children and particularly so for Traveller children. Most year 6 pupils have a visit to secondary school prior to starting in September and many schools have a programme of visits to help chil-

dren adjust to the differences and to meet key teachers. Because of their mobility some Traveller children may miss all this preparation and special arrangements may need to be made for them. Support with these arrangements may be available from an authority's Traveller Education Service.

Many Traveller parents have not attended secondary school themselves, especially beyond the age of 14. They often do not want their children to be exposed to what they perceive to be the more 'liberal' values of the wider society and are concerned to maintain their own cultural values. With little of their own practical experience to inform them, or with bad memories of the frustration of underachievement or bullying, they may be very fearful of what awaits their children.

Many parents and teenagers also find difficulty in understanding the relevance of the secondary curriculum to their intended lifestyle once they are able to read and write. Historically, and in many cases still today, boys are expected to spend time working with their fathers in an apprenticeship-style relationship and girls are expected to take responsibility for younger siblings and household tasks. Homework can prove very worrying. Working space and space for storing textbooks, equipment and schoolwork is very limited and parents, particularly if they are not literate, will be unable to give their children any help with difficulties.

Uniform codes of schools are usually very strict, and mobility can mean that young people would attend more than one school. Schools can assist by being more flexible about exact requirements or by lending or providing distinctive elements of their own uniform when needed.

> A secondary age Traveller girl writes about her educational experiences.
>
> *My name is N and I am twelve and a half years old. I was in a house in London for two and a half year and I used to go to school and I went for two years.*
>
> *When I first started school I was quite shocked. The two years flew on and I started to pick things up and I made lots of friends and I knew all the teachers in the school.*
>
> *I left the school to go to secondary school. It was right next door to it. I did not like it. The teachers were strict and they shouted too much. The teachers gave us detention if we did not do our homework and if we did not know how to do it, we still got detention. I never stayed long in school because we had to go out travelling. I wanted to go anyway. Then I came out travelling and I never felt better.*
>
> Noreen, age 14, in Essex in summer 1996

*Office for Standards in Education, 1996 *The Education of Travelling Children*, p 8

Induction Programmes

Secondary aged Traveller pupils who have little or no experience of formal schooling due to mobility may need a carefully planned induction programme which introduces them in stages to different aspects of the school organisation and curriculum. This programme would be time-limited and lead ultimately to full-time attendance. Such programmes need to be agreed with the relevant authorities, pupils, parents and support services, if involved.

Pastoral support in a school is especially important. Success in coping with such a large and complex organisation can hinge on the identification of a member of staff who will make him- or herself readily available to the Traveller pupils in case of difficulty. This member of staff would be well-informed about cultural issues, become known to parents as a link person and to teaching staff as a source of information, support and advice. Bullying and racist behaviour can be particularly damaging at secondary school level and schools need to closely monitor and evaluate their policies for dealing with such situations.

An example of a flexible induction programme

Two teenage girls, aged 13 and 14, had no experience of secondary schooling and fragmented primary schooling, due to a travelling lifestyle. They expressed an interest in learning to read. A local secondary school was very positive in its efforts to provide education for the girls.

The girls were taken on a tour of the school by Mrs B., the teacher designated for the care of Traveller pupils. The headteacher welcomed them and spent time choosing an appropriate tutor group, in year 8, where they could be together, and the two most appropriate days from the timetable to form an introductory programme. Some small group lessons, involving other Traveller pupils, were included in the two-day timetable.

The Traveller Education Service support teacher was encouraged to provide extra support on a flexible basis and was introduced to the staff members and to the resources available in the library for small group work. Uniform was discussed and the missing few items – ties and jackets – loaned from the school.

Two girls from their new tutor group were asked to meet the new pupils in the reception area for the first few days and assist them to settle into the routines of the school. Mrs B. alerted all the members of staff who would be coming into contact with the girls. The school had been welcoming Traveller pupils for many years and had a strong commitment to securing access to education for all its pupils, by using a variety of teaching methods, in-service training, especially for new staff, and by encouraging all pupils to support and help each other with their class work.

Teaching and Learning Styles

School subjects may become increasingly difficult to manage due to absences caused by family mobility. Support systems, both in the school and from Traveller Education Services become important in terms of helping young people with gaps in subject knowledge, supporting differentiation and helping parents to understand the demands placed on their children and the relevance of the school curriculum to their lives.

Organisational flexibility needs to be used positively to maintain the young person's attendance, making maximum use of options relevant to Traveller lifestyle. Pupils are expected to take increasing responsibility for themselves and make important choices. They need to understand that academic success is not the only benefit available in secondary schools. There is a widening of life choices and broadening of experience.

Particular skills and knowledge needed, when beginning secondary school, include the ability to read a timetable, an understanding of how to move around the school buildings, what is expected at dinner breaks, the importance of timing for registration, lessons and breaks and the need to bring their own specialist equipment to certain lessons.

Some secondary age Traveller pupils may be beginner readers. Copying from a white- or blackboard or from worksheets with a complex text may not be appropriate. Specialist support services may have a role to play but an awareness on the part of a subject teacher of the issues raised by beginner readers for teaching style may benefit many other children in a class, given that a variety of teaching approaches is needed to take account of a variety of learning styles.

It may be useful to consider:

- the level of language used in making key points in a lesson;

- lesson aims and purposes which are clear and limited to certain key concepts for some children;

- the use of pictures, short tape recordings and group or drama work or peer tutoring, so that key ideas can be re-visited in different ways;

- the possibilities of dictated writing as a means of recording;

- key sentences or ideas available in a simplified form on a sheet near the pupil to avoid the confusion of copying at a distance;

- that beginner readers, taught in an appropriate way, may grasp the subject lesson content but be unable to demonstrate this by recording in a conventional written form;

- special arrangements for homework, which is often a reading or writing task.

Pupils and parents talking about secondary school

"I want people to know what we're like and tell them we're not all wild and that people are different. I could stand up and speak to my English class because I had confidence in myself and that other pupils wouldn't laugh at me. In other schools if I did that they would laugh at me and call me gyppo – I've been called gyppo a lot by young children. I've never been called names here because C. [school name] has had Travellers a lot. The teachers all help me and don't make a thing about that I can't read much. They say they are sorry they can't help me more. Pupils always help me write things down and the teachers never mind."

Danielle, aged 14, at school in Essex, talking about her GCSE oral English exam

"Secondary school, no, I've never been inside one. When there's older children it's very embarrassing. They're in front of a class full of big children. They won't go any more because all these other children can read and write but the Traveller child can't. The other children laugh and say they're silly or stupid. It's not that they're silly or stupid, they just haven't had a chance, I mean nobody could read if they wasn't learned. J. [son] can read a good bit, since he was younger, so it wasn't so bad for him. He can read so it wasn't bad for him. He felt lost by himself. He said the school was very big. He felt a bit lost, he went on his own. When the future is coming, the travelling is coming to an end. Well, what I mean is, when we, they, have to move into

houses – what will happen to the children, when they get jobs – the children, when they come our age, when they can't read or write and they're people just like you, you know what I mean. They've got to think of things like that haven't they?"

Irish Traveller mother, with three teenage children, who travels seasonally

"When I knew I had to go to school I looked forward to it. But then, when I was in, I didn't like being there all day and sitting on hard seats. I was called names [by other children] and I hit them. Copying writing from the board was difficult because I couldn't read it.

This school is a good school. I'd like to get seven GCSEs, two languages. I'm doing Spanish. I'm going to teach myself Chinese. I'm going to go all round the world when I'm older, or I could be a steward [on a plane or boat]."

Billy, age 15, at school in Essex

"Really and truly you're lucky, more than lucky to get Travelling boys, 14 and 15, going to school anyway. My boys, it's only that I'm pushing them, because a Travelling boy, when they're 15, that's when they thinks of their life, how they've gotta live and how they've got to carry on. They're doubling, looking both ways."

Romany Gypsy mother, now living in a house, talking about her teenage children

This is our dog Queeny She is a Gerl

In the Classroom

Methods of classroom management and teaching which benefit Traveller pupils will also benefit many other pupils.

It may be appropriate to consider:

- **alternative means of getting information, other than by reading**
  detailed study of pictures,
  taped stories or accounts,
  short television, radio, video programmes,
  discussion in pairs,
  groups talking with one scribe,
  short talks by adults or children to the class.

- **alternative forms of recordings, other than by writing**
  labelled diagrams,
  picture sequences,
  drawings,
  photography,
  tape recordings,
  modelling.

- **making flexible use of others as support**
  bringing in parent helpers or teaching assistants
    on a short-term basis,
  using Traveller Education Support Teacher
    in a variety of ways,
  peer tutoring, now known to be effective
    in increasing retention of learning for both
    parties.

Remember that Traveller children:

- will often have less experience in reading and writing than their peers;

- may need time, in school, to experience what others already take for granted;

- have probably had experiences which may lead them to expect hostility from members of the settled community. Organising social support will be as important as organising curriculum support.

Top picture and picture sequence by Nathan, age 15

Peer tutoring has been shown by research to be effective in increasing retention of learning for both parties. It has been shown to be most useful when factual learning is involved or the teacher wants the pupils to learn a particular skill. *

A simple example would be a handwriting lesson. The teacher would demonstrate the correct letter formation to the class. The whole class would be paired so that each child who is a more fluent writer would partner a child who found handwriting difficult. The fluent writer would attempt the task first, with their partner watching, commenting and helping. The roles would then be reversed.

The child who needs most support with the task has three opportunities to learn. Once from the teacher instruction, once from checking the work of a partner, and once from completing the task him- or herself. The most able partner has the opportunity to demonstrate understanding and offer explanation of the task to another child and is therefore more likely to retain the knowledge or skill.

Peer tutoring can help to produce a non-threatening atmosphere, in which time on-task and independence is increased, whilst teacher input can be carefully focused. Incidental learning can also take place, such as mutual checking and correction of spellings, how to work in partnership with others and how to explain something clearly to another person.

Points to remember

- Children may not be confident about drawing. It is an activity with which they may have had little chance to experience.

- Traveller children have often learned a great deal by emulation and copying. Given the chance and plenty of encouragement, with good role models, they will do the same in school.

- Older children are used to taking responsibility in the home. They may appear more mature than many of their peers. However appearances can be deceptive. In the area of schoolwork, the children's self-esteem may be very low. Self-assurance can be masking a great deal of vulnerability and is easily shattered in the institutional world of school. Older children, particularly, will be very keen to be seen to be fitting in with the rest of the class.

---

*Goodlad S. & Hirst B. eds. (1990) *Explorations in Peer Tutoring*, Oxford, Basil Blackwell

The School Curriculum

Many aspects of the school curriculum will be unfamiliar to those Traveller children whose attendance at school has been fragmented by the mobility of their lifestyle. Here is a brief summary of some of the factors which schools need to be aware of, when planning and delivering lessons involving Traveller children.

General points

- Colour names may not be known by young children, descriptive names are sometimes used, for example, banana-coloured.

- Lack of access to drawing or writing materials, scissors or construction toys at home may mean fine motor skills have not developed as quickly as might be expected.

- Many conventions associated with the use of exercise books and paper will not be familiar.

- Many parents are extremely reluctant to allow their children to go on trips, organised for the class out of the school grounds, especially coach trips. This reluctance arises out of several factors: news on television about crashes and social isolation, combined with a protective style of parenting. It may take a long time to build up the necessary trust to gain their permission. If possible, it may be helpful to take along an adult Traveller or older sibling as a helper.

English

- Children's mode of speech and accent may differ from the majority of the class in the same way as a child moving from a different part of the country.

- Sitting, listening in a large group, at a distance from the speaker, is a 'foreign' experience.

- Older children may be able to recite the alphabet but have no knowledge of its significance.

- There is sometimes a complete lack of familiarity with the handling of books stemming from lack of experience.

- Nursery rhymes and traditional fairy tales may not be part of the culture handed down to Traveller children orally. Nursery rhyme books will not be familiar either, if parents do not read.

'Chip Wanted New Trainers' by Louise, age 8, at school in Essex April to June 1995

- Older children may not be able to read essential signs in the classroom and school. They can, however, often read signs associated with shops and the road, for example OPEN, CLOSED, SALE, STOP, GO, TELEPHONE, HOSPITAL. These are useful starting points, with relevance to their lives. Note that many signs appear in upper case letters, which are usually the most familiar to the children.

- If the children have been moving from school to school they may have been introduced to different basic reading schemes, causing confusion and loss of fragile self-esteem. Traveller Education support teachers may be able to advise the school of a reading scheme which is familiar to children, to maintain some consistency.

Mathematics

- Skills in mental arithmetic are often quite advanced. Once recording skills are taught, progress through the school curriculum can be very rapid, especially where the purpose of recording is clear.

- There may be a need for older children to have access to practical apparatus or have practical experiences to aid understanding.

- Children may not know how to name or use a ruler but may know a metal, retracting tape measure.

- Published schemes can be especially hard to access, as their particular conventions and need for reading often come between the child and the task.

Science

- This is often a popular and easily accessible subject, particularly the practical aspects. Formal recording skills will always need to be taught.

- Human biology can be a delicate area, as sex education is very often seen as a matter for the home. Traveller parents would usually prefer their children not to be taught about the physical aspects of sexual behaviour, or explicitly about menstruation and pregnancy. However the National Curriculum Science Programme of Study covers these subjects at Key Stage 3 and some elements will begin to be studied at Key Stage 2. Parents will need to be made aware, in a sensitive way, that human biology and reproduction are taught in the context of learning about life processes and the organisation of living things, alongside such matters as breathing, circulation and growth; whereas teaching about morals, values and relationships occurs within the Sex Education or Personal and Social Education programme.

- Do not assume any particular general knowledge, for example knowledge about nature because of an 'outdoor' lifestyle.

- Children may have had little experience of mains electricity but could understand a great deal about generators and other sources of power.

Art

- There is no tradition of providing materials for drawing as a play activity in many families. Children may be self-conscious about their lack of experience.

- Many children will never have had the opportunity to use paint, especially if attending school for the first time.

- Children usually love the opportunity to experiment with painting and modelling materials and may even like the clearing up afterwards, as a reason to use the running water!

Design and Technology

- This is often a motivating and accessible area of the curriculum, as its relevance to children's lifestyle can be easily grasped. Children often have a lot of knowledge about vehicles.

- There may have been a lack of access to commercial construction toys but children have often learned to be inventive with 'found' objects.

- Children may have quite comprehensive experience in the use of tools from an early age and parents sometimes have skill in a traditional craft, which they would be willing to share.

Drawing by Nathan, age 15, at school in Essex, December 1994 to February 1995

Geography

- Though children may have travelled extensively, do not assume they know how to use maps or have knowledge of the relative location of places.

- Usually the children's interest level is high in this subject and they may produce interesting oral descriptions of their experiences. Some children may not wish to draw attention to their nomadic lifestyle.

- In common with many other children, when they first attend school, Traveller children will probably need to be taught the precise meaning of some geographical vocabulary, for example stream, river, pond, lake, ocean, sea. Teachers need to be particularly aware of this when older children are entering school for the first time.

History

- Because some families lack firm identification with any particular country or local area, as do many other children, historical knowledge and skills are likely to be fairly sketchy.

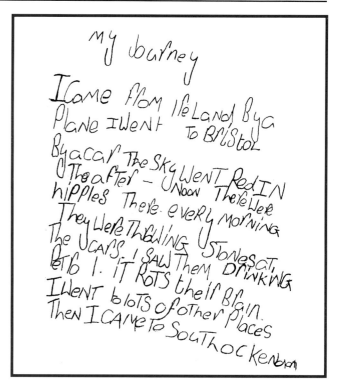

Story written by Paul, age 8, at school in Essex for periods between June 1994 and January 1995

- Some children may have interest in, or knowledge about the history of Travelling people but others may not see any relevance to the present. The history of Travellers can be brought into some historical topics in a quite natural way, for example when studying the Victorians.

Information Technology

- Children are unlikely to have opportunities to become familiar with computers or other devices which require a supply of mains electricity for use or charging.

Modern Foreign Languages

- The children may know some Anglo-Romani, Cant, Gammon or Shelta words but could be unaware of it, or consider the existence of an alternative language a family or community secret.

- Some children may be interested in using their knowledge of community languages to reflect on the different ways of expressing an idea in different languages.

- Children may know some German and be very interested in the language because increasing numbers of families are travelling there to work. As one 'English-speaking' Irish Traveller girl said *"I know some German, I speak Irish but my English isn't so good."*!

- The increasing tendency for some families to travel to France for religious conventions might also prove a strong incentive for learning French.

Music

- Children usually like singing, as this is an area of the curriculum where they can easily fit in. Sometimes it is difficult to understand 'practising' though. As one child put it *"Why are we singing, when no-one is listening?"*

- Do not assume knowledge of any particular musical tradition. For example Irish Traveller children may or may not listen to Irish music and know about the instruments involved. In common with other children, Traveller children are likely to listen to popular music on the radio and television.

Physical Education (PE)

- The PE curriculum can seem strange, difficult to master and embarrassing. One Traveller Education Service support teacher comments *"I will always remember the look of incredulity mixed with horror and disdain on the face of a seven year old boy,* *on his first day in school, being asked to join in with a music and movement lesson. 'I have to do that?' I had to admit, as I looked around the hall with fresh eyes, that it was very strange behaviour."*

- Some children, particularly from Romany Gypsy families, may be very embarrassed about changing in public for P.E.

- Formal team games, the use of mats, apparatus and specialist vocabulary in instructions may be confusing and physically difficult, until responses become automatic with practice. Complete withdrawal or boisterous showing off may be initial responses and this is understandable.

Religious Education

- Families are usually very happy to have their children receive religious education. Children's religious knowledge may be extensive, usually stemming from their parents' affiliation to a particular church and is likely to be derived from oral sources.

Drawing and writing by Margaret, age 10, at school in Essex January to April 1995

The Older Beginner Reader

Junior and secondary school teachers may have had no experience of teaching reading to beginners, or of teaching children who cannot read because of lack of previous opportunity to learn (rather than children who have a specific learning difficulty or who learn slowly). It can be very rewarding to teach such children because of the speed of their progress once they have got going, but initially, both the teacher and child may feel overwhelmed by the enormity of the task.

A child coming freshly to school at Key Stage 2 or 3 will need to revise or learn for the first time skills and habits of working which are normally taught in the reception year. Something as seemingly simple, or obvious as the convention which requires a worksheet or page to be studied systematically starting from the top left hand corner and scanning across from left to right and top to bottom, needs to be explained initially and then practised.

Children whose parents are not literate will have had few opportunities at home to hear stories read to them, to handle books, guess stories from the pictures, learn phrases and whole stories by heart or observe the many uses of reading and writing in everyday life. These experiences can be provided in school alongside the more formal learning of sight words and letter sounds.

There is a limit to the number of sounds or words that can be learnt in a week and the amount of time available to support one individual child's learning, even when others like the Traveller Education support teacher, special needs teacher, teaching assistant, parent helper and pupils in the class can help. However, when background activities are recognised as an important part of the reading curriculum, the task becomes more manageable and enjoyable for both teacher and child. The child will be able to do more short activities independently and be successfully completing achievable tasks. The teacher can feel reassured that a whole session 'just' looking at books or listening to taped stories or making a book from cut-out pictures is a developmentally appropriate activity. It may need to be explained to the class as a whole that the activities are not 'play' but appropriate tasks set by the teacher.

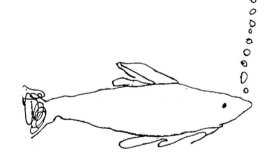

The River in Winter

Leaves floating down the river,
Weeds floating under water,
The water is bashing alongside the bank,
I can see the bottom,
I am freezing cold.

Fishing

How to catch a pike.
Things you need is
   a float
   and a hook
   and some ledger
   and some weights.

Picture and dictated poem by Danny, age 13

Reading activities could include:

- listening to stories read by another pupil;

- listening to taped stories;

- sharing books with a child who shares a similar reading level;

- sharing books with a child who shares a similar interest level;

- re-reading favourite books;

- looking at books alone or with a companion – picture books, non-fiction or fiction;

- drawing or tracing a character from a book;

- making books with cut-out pictures, drawings, tracings or patterns and having a scribe to write in the child's own words – titles like the following are often popular:

I like…	My favourite…	My family…
Me	My pets	My dog
Horses	Birds	My granny

- easy pop-up or lift-the-flap books, for example
  Where is the dog? In the tree.
  Where is the dog? In the basket…;

- repetitive humorous or nonsense books to learn particular words, for example,
  I fell off my bike,
  I fell off my chair,
  I fell off the table…;

- searching for and matching labels in the classroom;

- making lists, for example shopping list, lists of equipment;

- sorting and matching games with pictures, words or letters;

- making sentences with known words, particularly nonsense sentences, for instance 'mum is in the tree';

- making simple games like Lotto or Bingo for the class topic;

- cutting out words or letters from newspaper headlines;

- learning to spell words which the child has already learnt to read;

- points challenges, for example, five points for every word read without hesitation, four points if the word is worked out correctly, two points if the initial sound is known, building up to high scores with a lot of familiar words and a few new ones each time;

- timed challenges such as, 'How many words can you read in one minute?' or 'How long will it take to read this book? Guess first and then time yourself.' Often the task takes a much shorter time than the child expects.

The child's name and other family names may be a good starting point for early success in sight vocabulary. For instance if Mum, Dad, Jim, Rose, Caroline and Smith are already known, coupled with STOP and MACDONALDS from social sight words, a healthy looking score of forty points in the points challenge game could be achieved quite quickly.

When the number of sight words starts to get unwieldy, an alphabetically organised word bank, either written on a single A4 sheet or some sort of card index system is useful so that words can begin to be easily available for writing.

Revising and practising what is already known in familiar games and familiar activities can help increase both self confidence and independence. Class members can be encouraged to be actively involved in helping and supporting progress and benefit themselves in speaking and listening and social skills.

Some children may have learnt to spell out words by using letter names, for example N O spells no. Some may have learnt to recite the alphabet and recognise some of the letter shapes by name. Sixteen of the 26 capital letters are the same or very similar to lower case letters. If some capital letters are already known these can provide a useful starting point for learning further letter names and sounds and provide a much-needed boost to self-confidence.

A child's oral abilities and thinking skills are often much greater than might be assumed from their handwriting skills. Where children have missed significant amounts of infant schooling it is often helpful for them to be able to practise correct letter formation. In some cases tracing over letter shapes will be beneficial, especially for left-handed children or young Key Stage 2 children with little previous school experience.

For older children motivation to learn to read may be the most important consideration. **Children may be keen to learn to read using their own writings** about their interests such as football, recipes, soap operas, pop songs, road signs and learning to drive, boxing, or a particular aspect of the class topic or school subject like poetry or science. This type of approach allows early reading activities to blend in more easily with what the rest of the class are doing, which can be of overriding importance to some older children. Materials will be more suitable to interest levels and, where computers are available, children will be able to produce books of which they can be proud. Brigid Smith (1994) in her book *Through Writing to Reading* includes a step-by-step training program for volunteer adults working with young people on their own dictated stories.

Although schools place enormous emphasis on learning to read, a great deal of learning and life can take place without literacy. The older beginner reader will be able to take part in and contribute to many subjects, once access is opened up, by using methods which rely on speaking and listening, including verbal presentations, discussions, tapes, videos and help from peers and teachers with written instructions.

Blackberry and Elderberry Beer

Pick the elderberries by the stalks and put them in a bag with the blackberries.

When you get home, pick the stalk up carefully and run your hand down them and all the little things fall off. Squeeze them up in a plastic bag and put the juice in a bottle.

Add 3 or 4 spoonfuls of sugar. Do the same with the blackberries. Put the juice in the bottle and mix it all up.
If you want to you can put it in the oven but I don't bother with it.

When you get it out of the oven, put a little bit of beer in it.
Shake it and it all comes up fizzy.
Drink it straight away.

Dictated recipe by Billy, age 14

Drawing by Fred, age 13

A RABIT

HORSES

A GOOSE

A CHICKEN

A GUINEY PIG

CHAPTER 4

TRAVELLER EDUCATION SUPPORT SERVICES

This chapter explains the background to the development of Traveller Education Support Services and gives an overview of approaches to support which may be offered to schools and pupils. Some examples of successful continuity strategies, developed in response to family mobility, are also given.

Inter-agency working is important in helping Traveller families to gain access to a range of public services and background information is provided for professionals working with Traveller parents.

"A nomadic lifestyle inevitably creates practical difficulties for access to schools. Not all groups within the Travelling communities have historically been subject to prejudice or hostility. Nevertheless, even they often have to overcome difficulties that stem from the fact that they do not lead a settled life. It is, however, unacceptable that access for some Travelling children should be further hampered by open or hidden prejudice within the wider community or among Travellers themselves. It is perhaps ironic that while there is evidence of growing understanding and positive attitudes towards Travelling children in most schools, there are still many Gypsy and New Traveller families who harbour both anxiety and resistance towards education."

Ofsted, (Office for Standards in Education),
The Education of Travelling Children 1996

Accommodation and Education

Many Traveller parents desire schooling for their children and this is not incompatible with planned movement. However, the schooling of some children is affected by multiple disadvantages if, for example, families are being frequently evicted, parents are not literate and have had little, or no, school experience themselves.

Although large tracts of land are available for holiday-makers to live in static caravans, to move from site to site with touring caravans and for the storage of caravans during the winter months, Travellers have found that the realities of the planning process have left 30 to 40 per cent of the community without a legal place to site their caravans as they travel.

The 1968 Caravan Sites Act placed local authorities under a duty to provide sites for Travellers. In the Netherlands, the central government imposed a time-limit and designated a site itself if local districts did not provide one. In this country, the provision of sites has been patchy. The Criminal Justice and Public Order Act, 1994 removes the duty on local authorities to provide sites, although they should make provision for Travellers in their structure plans.

Some local authorities have to spend money on crisis management, legal fees and moving families temporarily elsewhere. For some families it means a

Drawing by Johnny, age 7, at school in Essex, June 1996

Drawing and writing by Shane, age 9, at school in Essex April to May 1995

constant round of evictions, accompanied by serious difficulties in getting access to health and education services. It also means that families have to cope with a debilitating label, which characterises their whole culture and lifestyle as anti-social behaviour, which is a drain on community charge payers. If the basic need for accommodation were to be met, it would enable Traveller families to pay rent and community charges and to access services such as education, in common with other groups in society.

It is easy to see the iniquities suffered by nomadic tribes in the Amazon or Aborigines in Australia. It is more difficult to be objective about nomadic people in our own society. Uninformed fear of strangers and envy of a lifestyle which is mistakenly perceived to be carefree and duty-free, is sustained by lack of information about actual people and their lives. The Travelling communities have no history or tradition of formal education, although they have survived as a viable workforce over generations, as a result of their strong and effective family education.

Central Government Support

Government has recognised the need for specific support since 1970, when a member of Her Majesty's Inspectorate (HMI) first became responsible for the overview of the education of Travelling children (Gypsy, Traveller, Fairground and Circus) and the first Department of Education and Science (DES) national short course was organised. Both the HMI Discussion Paper (1983) and the Swann Report, *Education for All* (1985) emphasised the need for accommodation as well as education.

At present, local authorities can bid for a grant under section 488 of the Education Act 1996, formerly section 210, Education Reform Act (1988), to help pay for their programme of support for the education of Travelling children in schools in their area. Grant-maintained schools can make individual bids to the Department for Education and Employment which, if successful, are then deducted from the local education authority grant. Traveller Education Services may support grant-maintained schools, some for a small charge and others free of additional cost. A network of Traveller Education Services provides some measure of continuity across the country, although there are gaps where authorities do not provide a service.

"Whereas with the other groups of children whom we have considered, we have been chiefly concerned with their needs within schools, many of the particular educational needs of Travellers' children arise because of difficulties in gaining access to the education system at all.

"In many ways the situation of Travellers' children in Britain today throws into stark relief many of the factors which influence the education of children from other ethnic minority groups – racism and discrimination, myths, stereotyping and misinformation, the inappropriateness and inflexibility of the education system and the need for better links between homes and schools, teachers and parents."

*Education for All :
the report of the Committee
of Enquiry into the Education of
Children from Ethnic Minority Groups.*
DES 1985

The Work of Traveller Education Services

Schools and families may be offered some, or all of the following types of support, aiming to enhance the quality of educational opportunity and raise the educational attainment of Traveller children:

- staff development opportunities for all school staff and other agencies;
- planned, collaborative or partnership teaching in classrooms where there are Traveller pupils;
- learning resources and materials related to Traveller lifestyles and experiences to encourage positive self-image in Traveller children and to broaden other children's understanding;
- support in forging relationships with Traveller parents;
- curriculum enhancement to all schools wishing to teach about Travellers, regardless of whether they have Travellers on roll;
- assistance to class teachers in differentiating between learning delay because of lack of opportunity and learning difficulties arising from special educational needs;
- closely focused support when Traveller pupils are transferring between schools, either because of family mobility or age;
- intensive support in the initial stages of admitting and integrating Traveller children from unauthorised encampments, who may have had little or no previous schooling, or be subject to frequent changes of school, both within and between local education authorities; support may be offered at the same time to parents to help them understand the routines and requirements of school attendance;
- advice and support in the preparation of distance learning packs for children whose families are seasonal Travellers;
- teaching support for the children of Traveller families who are mobile for part of the school year and are carrying distance learning packs;
- outreach work with Traveller families to encourage school attendance;
- help for schools in enlisting the support of governors and existing parents for an appropriate response to new Traveller pupils;
- specially trained, peripatetic classroom assistants;
- help to increase home-school contact, mutual understanding and the exchange of information. Specialist education welfare officers may be available to assist.

Children may need curriculum support because of:
- a late start to schooling;
- frequent breaks in schooling;
- a family background which may not have included school experience;
- parents who may not be literate.

Children may need social support in school because:
- they are members of a minority ethnic group, who are often subject to discrimination and prejudice;
- there may be great differences between the expectations of home and school;
- teachers may have little information on Traveller culture and history.

The Views of Ofsted

The Ofsted Report, *The Education of Travelling Children,* **was published in March 1996. The following points highlight good practice in a school's general approach to welcoming Traveller pupils.**

"Where the presence of Travelling children is openly acknowledged, and where accurate and positive images of the different nomadic communities are featured within both the resources of the school and the curriculum, then the response is lively and there is genuine openness to learning... schools have been significantly helped in this process by the work of Traveller Education Services which have provided the skills, information and resources... Where this is done well it has helped to improve the quality of learning and the accuracy of knowledge of all pupils." (point 38 p 18)

"Travelling pupils appear to achieve higher standards in schools which place great emphasis on equality of opportunity and, by encouraging the acceptance of cultural and ethnic diversity, establish an ethos which fosters self-esteem and pride in individual and group identity." (point 38 p 18)

"...Travelling pupils' achievements have been enhanced by a dual approach which focuses on improving literacy skills within the family as a whole. Such work... is effective in instilling in parents a greater degree of confidence to participate in, and contribute to, their children's education." (point 79 p 29)

Effective Support Teaching

Traveller Education Services throughout the country differ in the forms of support they offer to schools. However, larger services often employ peripatetic support teachers who work with schools in a variety of ways.

Schools offered support from Traveller Education Services may like to consider some of the ways in which this support could be used to raise the achievements and broaden the awareness of all pupils. Local circumstances will differ enormously, of course, according to the need and the resources available. Support may be targeted at the whole school, particular classes, small groups or, occasionally, individual children. Good practice in supporting Traveller pupils is also relevant to the needs of other minority ethnic pupils, as evidenced by the Ofsted Report *Education Support for Minority Ethnic Communities* (1994). In some authorities support for the education of Travelling children is part of minority ethnic or multi-cultural provision.

Whatever form of support is negotiated between a school and a support service, time allowed for joint planning and for regular review and evaluation is a crucial factor in maximising benefits to all concerned.

Some examples of approaches to class support are:

- working in partnership with a class teacher for mutually planned lessons, both teachers devising the programme together and complementing each other in the teaching of it, as noted in the Department of Education and Science and National Foundation for Education and Research (DES/NFER) Partnership Teaching Project, commissioned 1989;

- advising individual staff, teaching and non-teaching, on cultural issues which may affect learning, behaviour and day-to-day management;

- helping to adapt or differentiate curriculum materials that are being used by the class to meet the needs of specific Traveller pupils, or devising specially prepared materials which allow the pupils to work purposefully with their peers and encourage them to become independent of support;

- offering to loan or to create culturally relevant materials, which raise the awareness of all pupils and make the lesson more relevant to the Traveller pupils;

- teaching the rest of the class whilst the class teacher works with a child or group of children, or prepares distance learning materials;

- supporting initial assessment, so that the child can quickly be integrated into the work of the class at a suitable level;

- intensive short-term individual teaching programmes for pupils who have missed significant amounts of schooling, to meet clearly identified individual short-term needs;

- working with teachers to ensure that non-literate parents can understand school-home communications, for example by offering tape-recordings of end-of-year reports or to assist with homework. If needed, parents may be offered simple pictorial style letters for explanations of a pupil's absence from school.

Continuity Strategies

The distinguishing feature of the Travelling communities is mobility, past or present, for all or part of the school year. In order to maximise the quality of the children's educational experience, strategies which help to maintain continuity are very important.

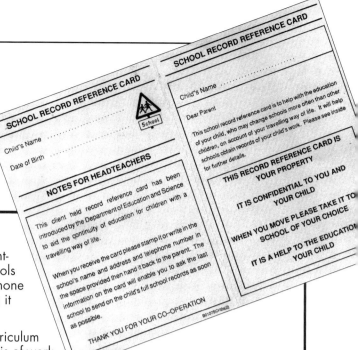

Examples of successful strategies

- The DfEE Record Reference Cards (Green Cards) are client-held aids to the transfer of records between schools. Schools need to stamp the card with the name, address and telephone number of the school and the date of admission, returning it immediately to the parent.

- The use of distance learning packs which continue the curriculum of a base school whilst travelling. These may form the basis of work in another short-term school placement or be supported by teachers from Traveller Education Services in the child's home.

- Short-stay Reports, devised by Traveller Education Services, can be passed between schools when families are having to move frequently. Such reports give a quick indication of the child's previous experiences to a receiving school, when a school's usual records for more settled children may not arrive before the children have to move on.

- Initial Assessments/Records of Achievement, devised by Traveller Education Services, can clearly and concisely indicate the child's achievements to a new teacher and ensure that work is set at the correct level, without the need for a new assessment period in each school.

- Continuity of personnel, where possible, particularly for outreach work helps to build up trusting relationships with families and realistic expectations and also supports strong home-school relationships.

- Speedy provision of discretionary home-school transport, where families are living in isolated or unfamiliar locations.

- Work with parents to encourage them to seek school places for their children themselves, immediately on arrival at a new stopping place rather than waiting for assistance. For parents, provision of contact numbers, information about procedures, and what to do in case of difficulties are all helpful. Support services can help by providing the same type of information to schools in their areas.

Distance Learning

Distance learning is a term which describes a variety of different styles of independent learning, away from an educational base. Although it is generally accepted that full access to the curriculum is best achieved in a school setting, it is recognised that in certain circumstances distance learning methods can be usefully employed.

For the children of seasonal, occupational Travellers a system of distance learning, managed by a winter base school in partnership with parents, provides educational continuity. The pupil can be provided with accessible modules of work from the teacher's schemes of work for the class and remain on the school roll while travelling.

The work can be presented using a wide variety of media: printed materials, computer programs, audio and video cassettes, radio and television. Within the framework of the National Curriculum the following features should help to make the work attractive to children working on their own:

- manageable units of work, attractively presented, for example, clear bold type, illustrations, plenty of space;

- bound booklets, which are much easier for children to manage than loose leaves;

- work which takes account of each individual child's needs, such as reading ability, and includes all necessary resources;

- a realistic time-scale for the completion of each module needs to be suggested and arrangements made for returning work to school for marking. New modules can then be obtained from school or posted.

Preparation of distance learning packs is most effectively organised by a teacher or small group of teachers within the child's base school, operating with clear guidelines. Support and advice may be available from a local education support service. A partnership with parents is essential to take into account individual circumstances and help them to organise the day-to-day management of their children's learning. Feedback from parents will be an important part of schools' evaluations of the success of the materials. Parents need to feel that their opinions, family skills and culture are valued.

One example of how distance learning can work

Sadie and Chantell are secondary pupils who spend October to March in a mid-Essex school alongside their peer group in the normal way. At Easter, they and their family leave their base for the summer season, taking their fairground rides and stalls to different venues throughout East Anglia. The school provides a varied and interesting workpack, which is exchanged several times over the summer, either by post or in person. The girls work on their pack daily and are supported by visiting teachers from the Traveller Education Services across the country. This ensures that continuity and work patterns are maintained. Sadie says "It keeps me up to date and it's much easier when we come back in."

Children may take their distance learning packs into different schools or receive teaching support from visiting Traveller Education support teachers. The packs should include records of work covered, with dates. Distance learning has been particularly important for Showmen's families. Most children return to full-time schooling in their winter base school, after a break of six to eight months. A lot can happen in those months, including playgroup friends starting school for the first time and older children transferring from primary to secondary school. Some children only attend school for a very short time if the winter season includes working trips abroad to fairs, in Dubai or Malaysia for example.

The education of circus children is likely to be organised in a similar way to that of children travelling with a fair, usually distance learning packs provided by a winter school. Larger circuses have sometimes had a teacher travelling with the children, organising their learning independently of a base school, but this is becoming rare in the United Kingdom.

Pre-school Education and Preparation for School

Because of the mobility of their families, many Travelling children will miss all, or part of, the vital reception year in school. In addition they may have had little or no opportunity to access pre-school provision. There is much regional variation, but average participation in any type of under-five provision for Travelling children, whose lifestyles range along a continuum from settled to nomadic, is only approximately 20 per cent. *

This low rate of participation is probably a combination of many factors arising out of lifestyle, culture and opportunities for access.

- The need for pre-school places on a short-term basis, which arises out of a partly mobile lifestyle, is difficult to cater for. Access is particularly difficult where places are in short supply and there are waiting lists.

- The location of sites, both authorised and unauthorised, away from housing areas can create transport problems where both parents are working and provision is part-time.

- When parents have had little regular schooling themselves they may need pro-active encouragement to see the value and relevance of pre-school provision in helping children to develop the skills needed in primary school.

- Families may feel that the children are too young to be exposed to education outside the family environment, or be unwilling to persevere in introducing children to pre-school experiences if the children are initially very reluctant.

- Where there is isolation from the settled population and restricted experience of pre-school within the Travelling community, accessing any provision without support can be a daunting task.

Some areas have recognised the difficulties for Travelling families in accessing pre-school education and have tried to address the need through inter-agency projects. Provision is geographically patchy. With the advent of the Nursery Voucher scheme, some parents will almost certainly be keen to find places for their four-year-old children and may need additional support to obtain both vouchers and places.

*Ofsted Report *The Education of Travelling Children 1996*

Inter-Agency Working

The isolation of Travelling families on unauthorised and some authorised sites, both geographically and socially, and the reluctance of many families to involve outside agencies in their lives if it is avoidable, means that access to public services is often restricted.

"Travellers' access to basic health-care provision in this country can only be described as tragic. Surveys in the Kent region* reveal that the infant mortality rate among Travellers is twice that of the settled community, and some 75 per cent of Traveller children do not complete immunisation courses ...
Travellers, like many ethnic minority groups, received a bad deal from the 1992 GP contract and face insurmountable problems in gaining access to the most basic services. GPs have to attain targets based on their lists before being paid for child immunisation and cytology. Many are reluctant to accept transient peoples on their list because if they move on, he or she will lose out financially. Even before the new contract, a post-reform survey of east London GPs** revealed that 10 per cent would not accept Travellers on their lists."

Christopher Tyler, *Travellers' Tale* in *Nursing Times*, volume 89, No. 33, 1993

The outreach function of Traveller Education Services has often meant that, in some areas, educa-

---

* Pahl, J., Vaile, M. *Health and Care among Travellers*. Kent: University of Kent and Canterbury Health Services Research Unit 1986
** Feder, G., *Traveller gypsies and primary care. Journal of the Royal College of General Practitioners* 1989, 39, 425-429

tion personnel are the only visitors to unauthorised encampments offering access to a 'service'. Some authorities have taken the initiative in establishing inter-agency liaison between all those with responsibilities towards nomadic communities, including the personnel responsible for site provision and representatives from community health services. This enables those visiting encampments to operate more effectively within their own area of expertise and ensures that Travelling families can gain access to the appropriate range of personnel and services.

Background Information for Professionals Working with Traveller Parents

It is difficult to generalise about the particular needs of Traveller parents. As in all communities, there are a number of distinct cultural groups and there are also wide variations between individuals within the same group. However it may be useful to be aware of some of the following general issues when working with families.

The history of Travelling communities has been characterised by nomadism, self-employment, oral transmission of culture from generation to generation, and strong family ties. Travellers and Gypsies are ethnic groups deserving of respect for their different lifestyle, customs and values. Their relationship with settled societies all over the world shows a similar pattern of discrimination, exclusion, low self-esteem, poor access to education and other public services, and a continuous pressure from authorities to 'settle'. Although nomadism may appear to be a matter of choice, for Travellers it is simply part of their culture.

I were going to my aunt Cathy's trailer.

I was climbing over the gate.

I fell off. I cut my eye on the concrete.

We went to the hospital.

I had an injection and three stitches.

Take great care of toddlers. They are more likely to have accidents.

Story by Linda, age 9

All families are different and will have had different life experiences, particularly influenced by the extent to which their life has had a nomadic pattern. Some Travellers are equally at home in settled society and Traveller society, have attended school regularly and are literate. Many adults cope extremely successfully without being able to read. On the other hand, regular travelling may have meant very fragmented schooling, experiences of falling further and further behind their peers and possibly bad experiences of bullying and prejudice. Good experiences and bad, passed down through the generations, affect each individual family's attitudes.

Extended family networks for support, in bringing up children and earning a living, are very important. Children have traditionally taken on adult roles far earlier than usual in settled society, the eldest girl becoming a carer of younger siblings and the eldest boy working with the men. Parents are extremely safety conscious and worry about their children when they are outside the Traveller community, even more so when they are outside the locality, on a school trip for example. This strong family and community support can be very reassuring, but can also at times have a restricting effect. If parents are reluctant to attend meetings or take part in other activities it may be helpful to consider extra outreach work, or ways of making social situations more comfortable, such as suggesting joint visits with other family members or friends.

Travellers and Gypsies have a very strong group identity. Initial time spent chatting and getting to know people's views, and allowing them to form their own opinions of you, can be important. Identify yourself before expecting people to identify themselves, make the purpose of your visit clear, and don't be offended if you are not invited into the trailer. This would be more intimate than being invited into a house.

If parents are not literate there will be a limit to the amount of detailed information that can be absorbed in one meeting. Materials which are intended to be kept and used for reference, or to be read and discussed later in private, will be of limited use. More visits may be required instead, to allow parents time to think about the issues involved. It is helpful to ask Travellers if they would like you to go through forms with them or act as a scribe.

"I'd love to know how to read – you lose out on a lot – if there's a letter or a form there's no privacy. We don't want the children to be the best scholars in the world, not to be doctors and nurses or anything like that. It's hard to see your own children not reading – we want them to read

– cos I can't read myself and it's so embarrassing. Everywhere you go you've got to sign your name to something. You go to the doctors and they give you a big form to sign and they say 'What – you can't read?!' "

Irish Traveller woman,
talking to a Traveller Education Support Teacher

Time may be measured differently. For example, a Traveller mother when asked if she had attended school as a child might say that she had, but on closer questioning it might emerge that she had only attended one school for a few days. The importance of keeping to exact appointment times may sometimes not be fully appreciated because of lack of understanding of the context in which professionals work. Some parents may be genuinely vague about exact days of the week, months of the year or dates of birth.

It is important to make your professional role clear to families. As with other communities some families may not fully understand the boundaries and rules governing particular professional activities. Travelling across county boundaries can compound confusion because of differing job titles, spheres of influence and procedures. Many families prefer to limit the extent to which they become involved with outside agencies to those which are strictly necessary. It may be important therefore to create, or open up, the possibility of a second visit. A refusal to become involved will often not be stated directly but politely disguised in a phrase such as "We're moving off tomorrow". On the other hand, large numbers of parents are pleased at the efforts made to reach out to their community and will ask directly for assistance in accessing public services.

Professional language and terminology, as is the case with many people, may not be understood. This may apply not only to the vocabulary used, but also to lack of knowledge of the practical context which give the words meaning. For instance the significance of phrases like 'learning words and letter sounds' will need to be explained with much more care to someone who is not literate. The more confused someone is, the more likely it is that they will be unable to ask any questions.

Different accents and turns of phrase may be difficult to understand at first. Family language, spoken quickly, may be intentionally impossible to understand. Travelling families may well speak their own language or dialect to each other in your presence. An aggressive or demanding attitude is quite likely to stem from feelings of anxiety or distress, combined with repeated experiences of hostility or rejection.

At the other extreme, some Traveller families may wish to withdraw from any situation which involves them with the settled community. "We're moving on soon" could be literally true, or could express a deeply rooted attitude. "We're moving to Scotland", that is, as far away as possible, would indicate very strong feelings of unease.

Spring and summer travelling patterns may need to be taken into account when planning a series of appointments, for example, educational psychologists managing the formal statementing process, treatment which is in short supply like speech therapy, and transfer to secondary school, where some arrangements have to be made nearly a year in advance. Travellers often have a relative living in a house or make arrangements to return to a site to pick up post or messages if they are convinced of the importance of keeping in contact.

Gender roles are often strongly differentiated. Neither women nor men will talk about matters of personal health when members of the opposite sex are present. These strongly held cultural taboos can influence relationships with doctors of the opposite sex, feelings about medicals and some aspects of the school curriculum like sex education and physical education, especially swimming. Hygiene rules are often strictly adhered to, for example different bowls are used for personal washing and for washing dishes. Tea towels may have to be washed separately from clothing.

If you are offered a cup of tea, don't put the cup on the floor or touch it after touching an animal. The cup might have to be thrown away! However on early acquaintance it could be important to take up the offer of that cup of tea. "I didn't think you'd take a cup of tea from a Gypsy" was one young woman's surprised response to acceptance.

"Travelling children… they're more grown up than settled children, they know a lot younger and they know how to look after themselves and take care of themselves. Some are settled but deep down they're all the same. They know they're Travellers, they know where they should be and where their people come from. They all know they're Travellers and they know how they're supposed to live. The worst thing for Travellers is sitting in the middle of people. They like their freedom and their open space. Say I'm living here, you got houses next door and people living in front of you. Now that's horrible. We like to live our own way, don't like to be gorja (non-Gypsy) all day… people looking at you, but that's just our own way of feeling. I like doors open, windows open, we don't like to feel all shut up."

Romany Gypsy mother, now living in a house

Nathan, age 15, 1995

CHAPTER 5

LEGISLATION AND TRAVELLERS

Readers will be aware that the law and its interpretation is constantly changing, as new cases reach the Courts and new legislation is enacted. However it is important to understand local education authorities' duty towards Travelling children, in the context of other laws affecting the lives of Travelling families.

This chapter gives a brief overview of current legislation in the United Kingdom, which specifically affects Travellers. Reference is also made to the importance which the European Union places on the preservation of cultural diversity and to the United Nations Convention on the Rights of the Child.

United Kingdom

Education

A local education authority's duty extends to all children residing in its area, whether permanently or temporarily.

"The duty thus embraces in particular Traveller children, including Gypsies." *

Local education authorities have a statutory duty to all children, including Traveller children, to make education available which is appropriate to their to their age, ability and aptitude, to enable parents to express their preference for a particular school and to meet any special educational needs the child may have. Parents are obliged to ensure that their child receives efficient full-time education suitable to the child's age, aptitude, or any special educational needs that he or she may have, while of compulsory school age.

A child must be *'receiving efficient full-time education... either by regular attendance at school or otherwise'* **. The majority of Traveller parents are choosing to educate their children within the State school system. However, as with the settled community, a minority of parents are choosing to educate their children, at their own expense, otherwise than at school.

---

* DES Circular 1/81 Paragraph 5 (an amendment to the Education Act 1980)
** section 7 Education Act 1996

Following the Criminal Justice and Public Order Act 1994, guidance was issued by the Department of the Environment and The Welsh Office, in Circulars 18/94 and 76/94 respectively *Gypsy sites policy and unauthorised camping*. The section concerning education makes these points in paragraph 11:

"LEAs should take careful account of the effects of an eviction on the education of children already enrolled, or in the process of being enrolled at a school. Where an authority decides to proceed with an eviction and any families concerned move elsewhere in the same area, alternative educational arrangements must be made in accordance with the requirements of the law appropriate to the children's ages, abilities and aptitudes."

Definition of 'Gypsy'

As far as the traditional Travelling community is concerned, Gypsy status is ascribed at birth. It is impossible to become a Gypsy and impossible to stop being one. A strong emphasis on family values, self-employment and the nomadic tradition also distinguish the Gypsy community. Whether a person could be said to be a Gypsy or not has also been significant to that person, in law. Legal Gypsy status depends on interpretation of definitions established in Parliament and in the Courts.

The definition of Gypsies in Section 24, Caravan Sites and Control of Development Act 1960, (amended by section 80 of the Criminal Justice and Public Order Act 1994) is:

"persons of nomadic habit of life, whatever their race or origin, but does not include members of a group of travelling showmen, or of persons engaged in travelling circuses, travelling together as such."

Relevant questions asked by authorities in determining Gypsy status have been:

1. Does the Traveller have links with other groups? 'Living and travelling together is a feature of nomadic peoples.'
2. Is there a pattern to the journeys made by the groups?
3. What is the purpose of the travel? *

It is, at present, for an individual authority (county or district) to decide on the facts of each case, which Travellers in its area are Gypsies, bearing in mind that

* Luke Clements, 1994, *Gypsy policy after the Criminal Justice and Public Order Act*. SAUS Gypsy Policy Seminar, Bristol

a **'nomadic habit of life'** may be seasonal or in abeyance. The Court of Appeal (R. v South Hams *ex parte* Gibb and others) 1994 has suggested that there should be a connection between wandering or travelling and the means whereby the Travellers make or seek their livelihood. Thus, Irish Travellers and New Travellers can fall into this definition of Gypsies.

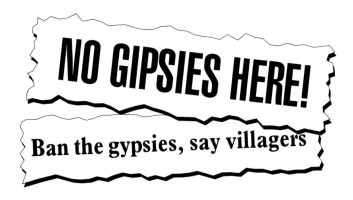

Examples of how newspapers often head articles concerning Travellers in a locality

How is Gypsy Status Beneficial in Law?

For those Travellers who wish to gain access to sites provided by local authorities, 'genuine' Gypsy status may be crucial. It can also be pertinent to the decision of a local authority officer who is deciding whether to evict, depending on the policies of the authority. Planning inspectors should also take Gypsy status into account.

A further important consideration simply rests on 'numbers'. The Department of the Environment requests figures, twice each year from local areas, of the numbers of Gypsy caravans pitched there. These figures do not include Travellers other than Gypsies, and are used for various statistical and sometimes political purposes. For example in the debates in the House of Lords on the Criminal Justice and Public Order Act *, the figures were used to show that despite the provision of more sites, between 1981 and 1994, the number of Gypsy caravans had increased and the number of unauthorised campers had also increased. The Government took the view that measures were needed, other than the provision of sites by local authorities, to eliminate the 'nuisance' of unauthorised camping.

The fact that more and more people appeared to be deciding to become nomadic ** meant that if all these people were to be allowed to fall into the definition of Gypsies, the arguments for increased provision of

* House of Lords Official Report, Hansard 11.7.94 Vol. 556, No 115 Col. 1524
** the increase in numbers of New Travellers as well as the Traveller population generally

permanent and temporary caravan sites would be greatly strengthened. The decision to be 'nomadic' was seen by Ministers as a matter of personal choice, which should not be supported by public money.

Travelling, for many families, permanently or seasonally, is an inherited and traditional lifestyle which they wish to maintain. However there is a large number of people who have taken up a travelling lifestyle for other reasons. Many New Travellers have made a positive choice to embrace an alternative lifestyle. However The Children's Society report *Out of Site, Out of Mind* (1994) states that:

"Two-thirds of the New Age Travellers involved in the study reported that they had been forced into travelling because of the circumstances they had been in. They included homelessness, family or relationship breakdown, leaving care, leaving prison, insecure housing arrangements, leaving the army, the need to escape from an abusive partner, and financial difficulties… Only two out of the 98 Travellers in the study stated that they had an existing alternative to travelling… There were no Travellers in the study who believed they had realistic access to current authorised sites."

Many New Travellers have children who have been born into a travelling lifestyle and for whom it is becoming an inherited tradition and culture. Organisations working on behalf of Travellers argue that the provisions of The Caravan Sites Act 1968 need to be restored, and extended to include all those people who genuinely depend on mobile accommodation as their only home throughout the year. At present the law effectively criminalises all Travellers without an authorised stopping place, whilst the reality is that there simply are not yet enough authorised public or private site places for those who need them.

Race Relations

The 1976 Race Relations Act gives legal protection to Romany Gypsies as a distinct ethnic minority group. The definition of an ethnic group is based on the elements of a long shared history, shared values and customs, lifestyles, traditions and other aspects such as a common language and religion. Direct discrimination is unlawful. Travellers are also covered in that some Gypsies are Travellers, therefore to discriminate against Travellers indirectly discriminates against Gypsies. For example 'No Travellers' signs, sometimes seen outside public houses, should be reported to the Commission for Racial Equality.

Examples of how public opposition to the establishment of sites is often reported in local newspapers

Accommodation

The Criminal Justice and Public Order Act 1994 makes it very difficult for Travellers to find a legal place to put their caravans and provides strong new powers to move families on, in some cases at very short notice.

- The Act removes the duty in the 1968 Caravan Sites Act for local authorities to provide residential or temporary caravan sites. However local authorities do have a power to provide sites if they choose to, and all structural plans should indicate provision for Travellers.

- In certain circumstances the Act makes it possible for families to be asked by the police to move at minimum notice, otherwise they will be arrested and the caravans impounded. They are not allowed back on that piece of land for the next three months.

- The Act presumes that Travellers will be helped by local authorities to provide their own private sites, but this is proving to be an almost impossible task. Planning permission is refused in over 90 per cent of cases *, and it is anyway a very expensive process.

This means that increasing numbers of families will probably find themselves on unauthorised stopping places and subjected to constant eviction, with no hope of a caravan site to live on.

---

* Sir David Mitchell House of Commons Official Report Vol. 241 cols. 315 to 320

By 1993 the proportion of families on the roadside had fallen to 33 per cent; unfortunately it is expected that this figure will rise. The Department of the Environment Count, January 1994, shows that, of 13,794 gypsy caravans counted, 4,118 had nowhere lawful to camp. The Government guidelines *Gypsy sites policy and unauthorised camping*, Circular 18/94, paragraph 6, gives very specific advice on not evicting unnecessarily and advises that:

"Where Gypsies are camped unlawfully on council land and are not causing a level of nuisance which cannot be effectively controlled, an immediate forced eviction might result in unauthorised camping on a site elsewhere in the area which could give rise to greater nuisance. Accordingly, authorities should consider tolerating Gypsies' presence on the land for short periods and should examine ways of minimising the level of nuisance on such tolerated sites, by providing basic services to Gypsies, for example toilets, a refuse skip and a supply of drinking water."

Housing Act 1985

Travellers with no legal place to camp are homeless under Part III of the Housing Act 1985. However many Travellers have no wish to move into housing and can face numerous difficulties, arising both from huge adjustments associated with lifestyle and customs, and prejudice from neighbours, if they choose to do so. The Code of Guidance (para 12.16) makes it clear that provision of accommodation under the Act will, in relation to Travellers, often entail the provision of a caravan pitch. *

The Children Act 1989

Local authority Social Services departments have obligations to Traveller families under Part III of the Children Act 1989, as they do to all families residing in their area. The difficulty in effectively meeting these obligations can arise where, because of successive evictions or threatened eviction, the families are highly mobile, even within a local area. Circular 18/94 reminds authorities of such obligations when considering evicting people from unauthorised or authorised sites.

Part III, section 17 of the Act describes the duty of a Social Services authority to safeguard and promote the welfare of children in need within their area. Section 20 includes the duty to accommodate any child, where a child's carers are prevented for whatever reason from providing the child 'with suitable accommodation or care.' This should not be seen as a threat to remove Traveller children from their families, as the underpinning philosophy of the Children

---

* Luke Clements 1995 SAUS Gypsy Policy Seminar 21.2.95 Bristol

Children In Focus – The Children's Society Magazine, 10.4.94

CHILDREN In Focus

News

ON THE ROAD TO NOWHERE

The Children's Society is appealing to the Government to:

In response to growing public concern about new age travellers the Government is clamping down on the people commonly described as 'scum' and 'vermin'. A new report published this month by The Children's Society reveals that this could be an attack on some of the most vulnerable members of society. Angus Stickler reports.

New age travellers are not just middle class drop-outs but homeless youth, care leavers and mothers escaping Bed and Breakfast according to a new report, *Out of Site Out of Mind*. Despite the threat of constant eviction and difficulty in obtaining the bare essentials to exist, travellers say they have created a lifestyle which offers them more than mainstream society.

"We were all expecting to find aggressive people living in squalor, taking drugs and 'raving'. But what we found were small, quiet communities. These are basically normal people and many were concerned that their lifestyles were being hi-jacked by ravers and people from the cities looking for a good time."

Young children make up a high proportion of travelling communities.

- consider the needs and safety of all children, including traveller children, as paramount in line with the UN Convention on the Rights of the Child;
- retain the duty on local authorities to provide sites and draw up toleration policies to avoid repeated and unnecessary evictions;
- recognise the opposition travellers face when attempting to obtain land in their own right and help them set up small transit sites with basic but adequate facilities;
- deny police the power to seize and destroy vehicles used as travellers' homes or means of transporting their homes.

Act is that, except in exceptional circumstances, children and their families should not be separated. *

Clearly in some cases, these duties to safeguard and promote the welfare of children, and to house the homeless, can place authorities in a difficult and conflicting situation when carrying out an eviction using the Criminal Justice and Public Order Act 1994. A recent judicial review (31.8.95) (sometimes called the 'Wealden Judgement') ruled that a district council and a county council were legally in the wrong when they failed to make proper enquiries about the welfare needs of the Travellers early in the process of deciding whether to evict them. Mr Justice Sedley said that the local authority had a responsibility to take into account:

"considerations of common humanity, none of which can properly be ignored when dealing with one of the most fundamental human needs, the need for shelter with at least a modicum of security." **

Europe

The European Union places considerable emphasis on providing for minorities, particularly migrant workers and Gypsies.

"Europe harbours many different cultures, all of them, including the minority cultures, enriching and contributing to the cultural diversity of Europe. A special place among the minorities is reserved for Gypsies. Living scattered all over Europe – they are a true European minority. As a non-territorial minority Gypsies greatly contribute to the cultural diversity of Europe." †

The European Parliament supports Gypsies in their quest for protection against discrimination. The Resolution of the European Parliament 24.5.84, paragraph 4:

"calls on the governments of the Member States to eliminate any discriminatory provisions which may still exist in their national legislation".

Many cases involving Traveller families are currently being taken to the European Court of Human Rights from the United Kingdom. The Committee of Ministers declared that:

"in their law and practice regarding the movement and residence of persons, States should refrain from any measures which would lead to discrimination against nomads for reasons of their lifestyle". ††

The United Nations Convention on the Rights of the Child

The re-drafted Rights of the Child came into effect in 1989. The United Kingdom government has signed it. There are 54 Articles, including the right to life, the right to a national identity, the right to the highest level of health care and the right to education. Article 30 states that the children of minorities, or indigenous population, have the right to enjoy their own culture and to practise their own religion and language.

The United Nations committee published, in January 1995, its report on how the signatories have succeeded in providing for their children. The section on the United Kingdom includes:

"In addition the committee recommends proactive measures for the rights of children belonging to Gypsy and Traveller communities, including their right to education and that a sufficient number of adequately appointed caravan sites for those communities be secured".

---

†† Lord Avebury quoting in House of Lords debate 7.6.94

by Albert

---

* Children Act 1989, Part-A1 288 Statutes, "… the prime responsibility for the upbringing of children rests with the parents and that the state should be ready to help parents to discharge that responsibility…"
** The Guardian 1.9.95 *Travellers' win makes Criminal Justice Law unworkable*
† Recommendation 1203 (1993) on Gypsies in Europe

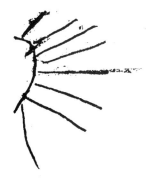

Once my brother never came with us to the plum orchard and my Dad bought an old trailer and my brother stayed in that.

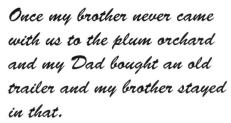

When the blankets were not folded up he went to bed, in the morning they were all folded up and the washing up was done.

It must have been an old woman who used to live in the trailer. I stayed with him for a day and I heard a noise like a chingling. WE WERE SURE IT WAS A GHOST.

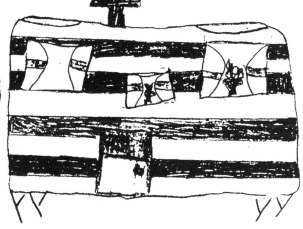

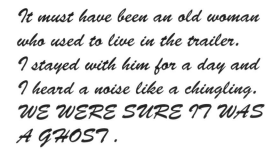

by Albert, age 13

CHAPTER 6

IS IT WORTH IT?

Examples of Work with Nomadic Children in Essex

In the course of our work with the children of nomadic or highly mobile family groups, we are often asked "Is it worth it, for just a week or two in school?"

An education of quality is a right for every child but can be particularly difficult to obtain for Traveller children. Travellers face increasing challenges in their everyday lives. If we exclude their children from access to educational provision then we participate in perpetuating the stereotypical images held by the Travelling and settled communities of each other. Lack of knowledge breeds intolerance and fosters prejudice and racial hatred. Education fuels acceptance of cultural difference and leads to greater tolerance and understanding, and is an investment in everyone's future.

An individual school may only see the children for a short time. By working in ways which facilitate the children's access to schools, promoting an increase in continuity of attendance, school work and records and through providing continuity of support personnel, the Essex Traveller Education Service has accumulated evidence which shows that it is worth it. Included in this chapter are some examples of children's work, extracts from teachers' records, reports and debriefing sessions with schools, and examples of success in countering fear, prejudice and hostility. They illustrate real progress in terms of access to school, academic achievement, and social and cultural enrichment for all.

Feedback from Schools

When a group of children has moved on from a school, it is part of our practice to debrief the headteacher and, where possible, the class teachers. They are asked for their views about the support we have offered, as well as being asked to comment in general about the experience of having Traveller children in their school. Without exception, these debriefing sessions have been a constructive experience for the peripatetic teachers involved. Feedback about the children has been very positive and most schools expressed regret at the shortness of their stay. One headteacher's statement encapsulates much of what we hope to hear in a debriefing session:

"… the experience of having Traveller children in school has broadened everyone's horizons and broken down barriers."

Other extracts from school debriefing reports:

"He makes you look at things differently; things we just take for granted, he asks questions about." (class teacher about Traveller boy in her class)

"They were very interesting. They told us a lot about how they lived and all the different schools they'd been to, and they spoke some German." (class teacher)

"For one little girl in the class Amanda was the first close friend she had made. She was heartbroken when Amanda had to leave and her mother took her to the trailer to say goodbye." (class teacher)

"… my initial anxieties about the children have proved unfounded." (headteacher)

"… sorry to see the children go." (headteacher)

> *"Our vision and our principles become worthwhile only when and if they are fully reflected in our practice."*
>
> *Every Learner –*
> *A Framework for the Curriculum in Essex*

DECEMBER

M T W T F S S
       1 2 3 4
5 6 7 8 9 10 11
12 13 14 15 16 17 18
19 20 21 22 23 24 25
26 27 28 29 30 31

JANUARY

M T W T F S S
              1
2 3 4 5 6 7 8
9 10 11 12 13 14 15
16 17 18 19 20 21 22
23 24 25 26 27 28 29
30 31

FEBRUARY

M T W T F S S
   1 2 3 4 5
6 7 8 9 10 11 12
13 14 15 16 17 18 19
20 21 22 23 24 25 26
27 28

MARCH

M T W T F S S
     1 2 3 4 5
6 7 8 9 10 11 12
13 14 15 16 17 18 19
20 21 22 23 24 25 26
27 28 29 30 31

APRIL

M T W T F S S
            1 2
3 4 5 6 7 8 9
10 11 12 13 14 15 16
17 18 19 20 21 22 23
24 25 26 27 28 29 30

Anne, Year 4, four different schools

DECEMBER

M T W T F S S
     1 2 3 4
5 6 7 8 9 10 11
12 13 14 15 16 17 18
19 20 21 22 23 24 25
26 27 28 29 30 31

JANUARY

M T W T F S S
              1
2 3 4 5 6 7 8
9 10 11 12 13 14 15
16 17 18 19 20 21 22
23 24 25 26 27 28 29
30 31

FEBRUARY

M T W T F S S
   1 2 3 4 5
6 7 8 9 10 11 12
13 14 15 16 17 18 19
20 21 22 23 24 25 26
27 28

MARCH

M T W T F S S
     1 2 3 4 5
6 7 8 9 10 11 12
13 14 15 16 17 18 19
20 21 22 23 24 25 26
27 28 29 30 31

APRIL

M T W T F S S
            1 2
3 4 5 6 7 8 9
10 11 12 13 14 15 16
17 18 19 20 21 22 23
24 25 26 27 28 29 30

Elizabeth, Year R, age 5 in April, three different schools

DECEMBER

M T W T F S S
     1 2 3 4
5 6 7 8 9 10 11
12 13 14 15 16 17 18
19 20 21 22 23 24 25
26 27 28 29 30 31

JANUARY

M T W T F S S
              1
2 3 4 5 6 7 8
9 10 11 12 13 14 15
16 17 18 19 20 21 22
23 24 25 26 27 28 29
30 31

FEBRUARY

M T W T F S S
   1 2 3 4 5
6 7 8 9 10 11 12
13 14 15 16 17 18 19
20 21 22 23 24 25 26
27 28

MARCH

M T W T F S S
     1 2 3 4 5
6 7 8 9 10 11 12
13 14 15 16 17 18 19
20 21 22 23 24 25 26
27 28 29 30 31

APRIL

M T W T F S S
            1 2
3 4 5 6 7 8 9
10 11 12 13 14 15 16
17 18 19 20 21 22 23
24 25 26 27 28 29 30

Miles, Year 3, four different schools

DECEMBER

M T W T F S S
     1 2 3 4
5 6 7 8 9 10 11
12 13 14 15 16 17 18
19 20 21 22 23 24 25
26 27 28 29 30 31

JANUARY

M T W T F S S
              1
2 3 4 5 6 7 8
9 10 11 12 13 14 15
16 17 18 19 20 21 22
23 24 25 26 27 28 29
30 31

FEBRUARY

M T W T F S S
   1 2 3 4 5
6 7 8 9 10 11 12
13 14 15 16 17 18 19
20 21 22 23 24 25 26
27 28

MARCH

M T W T F S S
     1 2 3 4 5
6 7 8 9 10 11 12
13 14 15 16 17 18 19
20 21 22 23 24 25 26
27 28 29 30 31

APRIL

M T W T F S S
            1 2
3 4 5 6 7 8 9
10 11 12 13 14 15 16
17 18 19 20 21 22 23
24 25 26 27 28 29 30

Margaret, Year 5, five different schools

Dear

[Mrs.] H ——————,

24ᵗʰ march

please read this out to the class.

I couldn't write bake to you because I never had eny posteg but thank you for yours eny way I am getting on very well + can do my X tables + I am the oldest in my class.
I am on the higest reading groap. Ann does not no I am writing this I wish I could be ther I miss you all I will try to write again. Love Ann + margaret + hellen

all our wishis. good by.

Copy of letter from Margaret, age 10, to a previous class in an Essex school. She attended five different schools in the county between January and April 1995

Attendance Patterns

The examples opposite show the attendance patterns of four children while they were at school in Essex. The shading refers to different schools. Despite evictions from up to eight different encampments in the county, the children were able to spend significant amounts of time in school. They were encouraged to carry their work on from school to school.

Evidence of Progress in Learning

To the right is an extract from the Traveller Education Service record which follows children from highly mobile family groups from school to school while they are in Essex. The record can also be sent to other local education authorities on request. This part of the record shows Ann's progress in learning sight vocabulary and her increased knowledge of phonics between December 1994 and March 1995.

5/12/94 5. Letter names and sounds

sight words: Ann,
doesn't appear to know any initial sounds.

3/2/95 5. Letter names and sounds

sight words: Ann, Helen, a black box in is the

24/3/95 5. Letter names and sounds

sight words: Ann Helen a I in is it It on no No to too took Mum Dad Floppy Kipper and the

Writes own name : **miEh**

Date: 19 . 1 . 95

Writes any other words or letters unaided : **ÞPMihXhOHA †**

Miles can ride a motorbike.
miles cah rLdea motobike.

Reading: Tells a detailed story from the pictures. He says he "reads" the pictures". Knows how to handle books and enjoys them.

Recites numbers to : 30

Counts to : 11 (using objects.

Writes numbers to :

Pencil held correctly. Letters and number mostly formed top to bottom.

rsefZ67&ℓ 1011055ɛ\P1h 161Γ18ℓ 150

Above is an extract from a quick assessment for Miles, age seven, completed on his first morning in school in Essex in January 1995. Miles attended four different schools before moving out of the county in March.

As part of evaluating our project with children from highly mobile families a similar assessment (opposite) was undertaken, as soon as it was known that Miles would be leaving the county. The resulting information was then shared with Miles to show him his own progress over the two months and communicated to his parents to encourage them in their efforts to gain as much schooling as possible for their children.

One Example of a School Transfer

Parents had informed me, the Traveller Education Service teacher supporting mobile groups, of their new location immediately on arrival, by pager message at 8.30pm. When I arrived next morning, two parents had been to the school to seek places for their children and had informed the school of our involvement. The headteacher had been able to seek information from me and from the children's previous schools that morning.

The children's work and records from these schools were then passed immediately to their new class teachers and, with the continuity of support teaching, the children had been able to settle very quickly into work in their new classes.

The children's stay had been short, partly due to the half-term holiday and partly because of an eviction. However, their entry had been so smooth that the children had been able to learn, even in such a short time.

Writes own name :

Miles D

Date: 21. 3. 95.

Writes any other words or letters unaided :

tA
ANNEN
HeLEN
bad
MyM
Dad M
Kipper
BbeA

Reading:

Reads Oxford Reading Tree Stage 2 books quite fluently and can recognize key words out of context. Using initial sounds he knows to help him.

Writes numbers to : 1 2 3 4 5 6 7 8 9 10 11 12 13 14 15 16 17 18 19

Other number skills : 20 21 22 23 24 25 27 28 29 3 3

Addition and subtraction to 20 without objects. Just starting to learn tens + units.

Elizabeth started school, for the first time, just before her fifth birthday in January 1995 and attended this school for eleven days.

The rest of the class had been in school for a term but the class teacher allowed for Elizabeth's different circumstances by arranging plenty of time for her to play in the home corner and gain her first experiences of sand-play, water-play, and other toys and equipment already familiar to the other children.

Below is part of the class teacher's report, which was passed on to Elizabeth's next school.

On the right are some extracts from the support teacher's notes. By this time Elizabeth was attending her fourth school in three months, though still in her first term in a reception class.

13.3.95 The classteacher says she has settled in really well. She just joined in with what all the others were doing. She definitely looks like a school girl in her uniform, is very composed and at ease and knows how to behave in school.

16.3.95 reading Story Chest. 'Copy-cat'. Didn't appear to be concentrating on the story. Probably needs grey Oxford Reading Tree for discussion and talking about pictures.

18.3.95 reading Story Chest. 'Copy-cat'. Amazing improvement, pointed to the words, remembered some of the phrases, told the story.

22.3.95 reading 'Mouse', 'Horace'. Listened intently to the story. We had a detailed discussion about having baths.

In spite of all the changes of school, Elizabeth was very happy and settled. Each short stay was obviously worth it.

10.2.95

Elizabeth was keen to write, in her own book, but as yet has only pre writing skills. However in the short time that she was with us her pencil control improved & this was shown in her "colouring in" skills. Elizabeth also likes to paint, and enjoys cutting and sticking.

Elizabeth enjoys looking at books, especially on a one to one basis and can listen attentively to a story.
I enjoyed Elizabeth's brief stay in our class and I wish her well for the future.

Examples of Success in Countering Fear, Prejudice and Hostility

A welcoming attitude and a willingness to confront misinformation

The headteacher, Mrs H., had seen the welcoming of this group of 12 nomadic Traveller children as an opportunity for her school community to widen their experience of other lifestyles.

Mrs H. had visited the temporary encampment a number of times. Two members of her staff and two nuns had also made a visit. She mentioned the calm atmosphere and feeling of safety she had experienced at the encampment, contrasting this with her fears of violence on inner city estates. She also noted the heavy police presence at the encampment. Mrs H. said that her visit to the site had helped her enormously in understanding the needs of the children who she was accepting into her school.

The school had experienced at first hand the power of negative stereotypes. Some children thought that one of the Traveller children had a penknife in the playground. This was thoroughly investigated and found to be completely untrue, but the rumour spread like wildfire and numbers of parents contacted the school the next day. Mrs H. spoke strongly to every class in the school, inviting them to imagine what it was like to be continuously moving from school to school, and the educational and social effects of this. With the older classes a game of Chinese Whispers was played to show how inaccurate information can spread. She exhorted all the pupils to make the Traveller children welcome in a Christian manner. I was able to feed back to Mrs H. that this strong moral lead had made an immediate difference to the atmosphere in the school.

Mrs H. took up the offer of a loan of books to raise awareness among children and parents of Traveller lifestyles. She used these in a short series of assemblies after the Traveller children had moved on.

It's horrible being a Traveller because you go all round the world and you meet new friends and you have to leave them.

The only reason I like a trailer is because it's comfy. The most goodest thing about a trailer is because you have a kitchen where you can eat in the morning.

We have bunks, four bedrooms and a dine-ess.

These are the people that live in our trailer. Their names is Jay, Mummy, mi Daddy, mi sister Nanny-Girl. I've got a dog called Patch and a dog called Sambo.

Dictated writing by Mary, age 8,
at school in Essex in January 1996

Circle Time: fostering self-esteem and pride in individual and group identity in school

Circle Time, or sharing time, takes different forms in schools, but generally involves an expectation that the pupils will listen to each other with respect. Sometimes children speak to the whole class and are asked questions, or each member in turn may tell about something that has made them happy, sad or frightened, for example. In this way an opportunity is provided for individual children to express their feelings as a natural part of class routines and to feel personally valued.

P., a Traveller child, was able to say to the class that, after initially being worried about break times, he was now quite happy in the playground. The other children were able to ask why P. always went over to the infant playground to see his little sister, which was normally against the rules of both schools. He explained that he needed to look after her. The support teacher was able to explain further that an exception was being made for a few days in P.'s case, as both schools understood his strong need to do this because the children were frequently moving to new schools. The class accepted the explanation with interest and understanding, some children contrasting P.'s need to be protective with their own desire to have a rest from the demands of younger siblings.

J. was finding great difficulty in settling into his class and making contact with other children. Through outreach work with J.'s family the support teacher knew that J. had a pet goat which travelled with them and that the goat had just had a baby. At sharing time the class teacher was prompted to ask J. about his news. For the first time he answered questions, volunteered information, listened attentively to a story about The Three Billy Goats Gruff and later drew his first picture.

*'The Three Billy Goats Gruff'
by Jim, age 8, at school
in Essex June and July 1996*

Including Traveller children's experiences as part of the normal variety of experience within the school community

When the presence of Travelling children is openly acknowledged by the school, in the content of lessons and in resources, the pupils are likely to be reassured that they are fully accepted.

In one school three children, all in different classes and in their first few days at the school, were asked if they would like to create a display about their travelling life, as so many people were interested. They set about producing work enthusiastically which told the whole school about what they liked best and least about a travelling life and about their recent celebration of Holy Communion.

> *The communion dress was all flowers with pearls and diamonds on. It was too long for me. My dress was long to the floor, and when I got out of the car I had to lift it up because I couldn't walk. I had high-heeled white shoes. It was nice wearing it because it felt good on your body.*

*Ann, age 9, at school in Essex in January 1996,
dictated writing and drawing*

Two secondary age Traveller girls were being taken on a tour of the school, before enrolling, by the Head of the Religious Education department. They were pleased to notice a display in a prominent position near the library which included, among other things, a large photograph of the inside of a trailer, some work by Traveller pupils in the school, and a Bible story booklet translated into Romanes.

A group of nomadic primary age Travellers were similarly reassured as they came into a new school by a 'Going Places' display in the entrance hall which happened to include two books about travelling lifestyles – *A Traveller Child* and *A Fairground Family*.

As part of a science lesson about electricity at Key Stage 2, when the class were discussing where electricity comes from, T. was able to contribute detailed information about a generator as a source of electricity. He knew how much fuel was needed, how much it cost to support his household's needs, and which appliances used gas and which used electricity.

During a history lesson at Key Stage 2, the class were comparing a Saxon dwelling with their own homes. This naturally led to a wider comparison between arrangements for sleeping, eating, cooking and washing in houses, flats, trailers (caravans) and Saxon homes.

As part of a Key Stage 1 maths lesson children were compiling a pictogram of class pets. This led to J. telling the class about his canary, puppies, the horses which his father breeds, and their new foal.

When encouraged to take part in a class discussion about holidays, in a junior school, three Traveller girls were able to tell the class how their families had been living and working in Germany for the last few months. They were able to relate their everyday experiences and to demonstrate their knowledge of German to the other children.

English GCSE Coursework

Life on the Fairground

A showman's life is very different from other peoples'.
Most showmen live in big caravans called trailers. Most trailers have at least two bedrooms, a kitchen, a living room and sometimes a bathroom. My family's trailer is 40 feet long and about 12 feet wide. We live in it all the year round. In winter we are parked up in the showman's winter quarters. This is a big yard where we can also repair or replace any of our equipment that needs it.

At Easter we pull out. This means we move off to our first ground – the place where the first fair will be held. We tow our trailer with an ERF lorry, and we usually go to Hampstead Heath first. The summer's run (our route for the season) is mainly decided in advance and is roughly the same from year to year. We either stay a week or a fortnight in each place. When we arrive it's called pulling on. When we leave it's called pulling off.

When we get to each ground we set the caravan, which means we get it in the right position and level. Then we unpack everything in the caravan which had to be stored safely while we travelled – glass, china, the TV, etc. After we have set the trailer we set the lorry, because the lorry has the ride on it. By this time we've usually had enough for one day, what with the journey and everything else, so we leave it there and get up early the next day and start putting the ride together.

The first thing we do is unpack the clutter. Then we level the centre and then we put up the arms which is the main structure of the machine. They have to be securely put up with big bolts. Then we put up the crossbars, which also help the structure and keep it in place, stopping it moving about. The next thing we do is put the elbows on. They are bolted on to the ends of the arms. Then we put the light strips on the arms and on the 'bows'. Next we slot the umbrellas on, and then we take down the platform which we stand on to put the main part of the machine up.

We put on the 'bananas'. These are banana-shaped lumps of metal which hold the cars on. The cars are bolted to the bananas and tightened. Then we put the 'scenery' up – that's the front of the machine. It's the cash desk and the gates, which go round the outside of the machine to keep the people away from the moving parts. The ride is called the Paratrooper Ride or the Umbrellas. Then we are ready to 'open'. This means the fair is ready to start.

When we have finished the place, we have to 'pull down'. This means we have to do everything again, in reverse. That usually takes all night. Then we have to get up early to travel to the next place. Sometimes this could be very near, but often it could be 100 miles away.

I enjoy the summer because I see more of my mates, but it's hard work. We make up for it though when we can, after the fair shuts. We usually stay up very late having a good time.

Vernon, at school in Essex 1996

Including Traveller experience in an inter-cultural curriculum for all children

Knowledge about other cultures and ways of life encourages respect for others, reflection and a deeper understanding of today's complex society. Where teachers incorporate this knowledge into their curriculum planning and day-to-day lessons, it becomes a natural part of children's learning. The following are examples of Traveller experience being used to enrich the curriculum for all pupils, whether Travellers are on the school roll or not.

Water: Working with a class teacher on her planning for the term's topic on 'Water', a support teacher provided background information and prepared materials for the whole class which introduced aspects of Traveller culture and day-to-day experience. The lessons included slides and pictures of trailers to highlight Traveller use and storage of water. A consideration of life without clean, running water on tap led the class into thinking carefully about their own everyday uses of water, where it comes from, where it is stored, and how much is used. Science experiments were carried out to see which materials would be best for storing water and why. Mathematics work was undertaken on the capacity of water containers. The class were invited to experience how heavy water is to carry, so that they could consider the difficulties of managing with only as much water as could be stored and carried. The class were also introduced to the life of Bargee families in an historical context and to some traditional decorative patterns to use on the model barges which they made. The final lesson included a general talk about the life of modern-day Travellers from a variety of communities, and led the class into thinking about why there is so much prejudice. They were asked to imagine what it would be like to travel from place to place frequently and what aspects of their lives would be affected.

Media Studies: In response to requests from secondary schools Traveller Education support teachers collected together a number of materials, some focusing on a particular incident experienced by a small group of Travelling families.

1. I was asleep in my bed when someone threw a stone at my window.

2. I looked out from the window. There was men fighting.

3. My dad called the police on our phone.

4. The police came. Eight men was arrested and a lot went to hospital.

5. We had to leave that night. We went to the hospital. We waited till our men got out.

6. They had to go to court. Everybody had to go to court.

not guilty

Tommy

The materials included:

- accounts of the same incident from a number of different newspapers;

- a dictated account by one of the Travellers involved of her perception of events;

- a pictorial account by one of the Traveller children;

- letters written by settled children in their class the following day, saying how they felt about the incident happening in their community;

- background information about Traveller lifestyle and culture, some from newspaper accounts;

- extracts from local newspapers in other nearby areas where the same group had been stopping.

Playground and dining hall support

Children can be supported to gradually build up the skills they need in new and sometimes frightening social situations.

M., who had just started in the reception class at a new school, was refusing point blank to go out into the playground at playtime, or to go into the dining hall. Later in the week she was able to articulate her fears – "These are not my people, I'm feared." In the beginning all she could do was cling onto the furniture and say no. When she first opened the door into the dining hall the sudden rush of noise and mass of people made her literally fall over backwards.

The Traveller Education support teacher was able to help her overcome her fear of playtimes by teaching her playground games. Other children in the class were keen to join in 'The Farmer's in his Den', 'In and Out the Dusty Bluebells', 'The Princess Lives in a Big, High Tower', ball games and skipping games.

M.'s fears about the dining hall were explained to the school staff who had been unsure how best to deal with her behaviour. One midday assistant was enlisted to support her through the process of queuing and choosing her dinner. For the first two days she also sat with the children at the table whilst they were eating. On the third day M. was first in the class queue for dinners.

In the dinner break J. snatched stickers from two infant children. Other children came to their aid and were ganging up on him. J. listened when the support teacher explained how upset the little boys were and asked him to consider how he could make amends. He decided to give them back two stickers each, giving them two of his own. J. was amazed and delighted to see the pleased expression of the two little boys as he gave them the stickers. He had been encouraged, in a very practical way, to explore a different response to a threatening situation.

Assemblies: enabling children to reflect on, and change, their attitudes and behaviour.

Assemblies provide an opportunity for consideration of issues which affect the whole school community within a broad spiritual, moral, social and cultural framework. Consideration of relationships with others, both within and outside the school community, forms a natural part of the subject matter.

Eight Traveller children started at a school at the beginning of July. Their arrival caused something of a stir among the children and parents. The deputy head decided to hold an assembly on the theme of 'Starting School' which acknowledged the presence of the new children and welcomed them. She invited the other children to look back and remember their own feelings at the beginning of the new school year and that rules which were now very familiar had had to be learned. Everyone was invited to suggest ways of helping the new children settle in. No direct mention was made of the fact that the children were Travellers, instead emphasis was placed on the things which all the children had in common.

Providing information, training and resources

All members of the school community, including non-teaching staff, benefit from information and training which help them respond sensitively to new Travelling children within the framework of their own schools' policies.

An illustrated loose-leaf pack, containing information about the Travelling communities, their lifestyle, history and culture and other information to aid successful integration into school life, has been made available to schools accepting nomadic Traveller children. It has been kept in staffrooms and dipped into with interest by class teachers, headteachers, midday assistants, school secretaries and teaching assistants. In a lot of different schools it has provided a stimulus to questions and discussions, and has changed perspectives.

The information pack has also been used in more formal in-service training for schools and other professionals. One school was preparing for a group of new pupils from a newly-opened site. The local community had been very hostile to the site being built in their area. Protest demonstrations had been held, letters sent to the press, and the Chairman of the Governors approached repeatedly by protesting parents. Staff were aware that settled children were likely to be coming into school having heard hostile comments at home and in the media.

At a small village school, the arrival of a new Gypsy family from the nearby site caused a lot of hostility to be expressed by the Parents' Association. The headteacher requested help from the Traveller Education Service in reviewing the school's equal opportunities policy and in preparing and holding some assemblies for the whole school. The assemblies included material from *You, Me, Us! – Social and Moral Responsibility for Primary Schools.* * The section 'Respecting Differences' includes a story about the friendship between two children, one a Traveller, who are not initially accepted by the others in their class, and emphasises how the two boys feel about their experiences in school. The story is told through the eyes of one child with the aim of increasing all children's understanding of what it feels like to be isolated and rejected. Ideas for discussion are included with the story.

Three separate preparatory training sessions were held for dinner ladies, teaching staff and governors. The 'Midday and Playground Assistants' sheet from the information pack was given as a handout to each dinner lady and two information packs were given to the school, one to be available in the staffroom and one for borrowing by individual members of staff.

A pack of laminated A4 photographs of the building of the site was also given to the school as a curriculum resource. The pack provided attractive visual aids which would naturally include the Traveller children's experience in a number of different curriculum areas.

A teacher from the Traveller Education Service supported the school on the first day, when the new children started, and noted that the playground assistant was confident in dealing sensitively with incidents of name-calling.

As so often happens, the Traveller children were their own best ambassadors.

---

* Rowe and Newton, Citizenship Foundation 1994

When one year 6 girl moved on, her classmate wrote on the bottom of her card –
'COME BACK, WE MISS YOU'.
A younger boy said of his Traveller classmate,
"We didn't know he'd be like that, just like us."
A teacher commented *"The [Traveller] children were so polite. Much more polite than many of the other children here."*
A dinner lady said *"It's so sad they've gone, they were lovely children. We've missed them. When the new ones start, we'll do our best with them, you know. We always do our best."*

All the children are in school.

Changing prejudiced attitudes by involving parents

Face-to-face contact between people is likely to be the most effective way of challenging any preconceived ideas. The school is part of the wider community and a natural place for people to meet and get to know each other, with the common purpose of supporting a broad education for all the children, in various ways.

In a small village school the headteacher is pro-active in encouraging Traveller parents to visit the school and become involved whenever possible in its activities.

The first step was to encourage Traveller parents to accompany school trips and visits, as parent-helpers. This enabled other Traveller mothers to feel confident enough to allow their children to take part. The next stage was to involve one mother in accompanying the pupils on their weekly visit to the swimming pool. This solved potential problems about changing in groups.

When the school was doing a topic on levers and wheels, the headteacher arranged for the parents of one child to bring their horse and cart to school. The pupils were able to hear about the parts of a vehicle, see how levers were used and have rides around the field. This led to pony rides being available at the next school fête and also a wagon being on show. Care still had to be taken with preparations for the event. Many parents had made great progress in confronting their own prejudices but it would be wrong to force the pace.

Traveller parents often have skills which many would find difficult to copy, even poorly. One parent was skilled at making paper flowers and brought some as a contribution for the Christmas Bazaar. They sold well and were much admired. As a result she was asked to demonstrate the craft in class. Careful persuasion, encouragement and confidence-building were necessary. There were also some disparaging remarks and scepticism prior to the day from some pupils. However once the talk and demonstration had produced a rose and a carnation, the class were more appreciative of the skill involved. As they began to make their own, they discovered how difficult it was to make anything look like a flower, never mind a recognisable rose or carnation. *"Ye-e-es, but is it a rose or a carnation?"* was a typical question heard around the class!

The appreciation and respect for that mother increased enormously. A wide range of skills relevant to the curriculum had been demonstrated, taught, practised and learnt. The pupils also each learnt a lot about personal relationships, perceptions and respect, and noticeably gained in maturity.

The flowers were on display at an open evening, decorated the table at a governors' meeting, and were taken as posies in baskets to sell to visitors at the 'Victorian Dress Day' at the local railway museum. The income more than paid the fares of the children whose parents could not afford the cost.

Conclusion

"Is it worth it?"
The answer to this question really depends on who is doing the asking.

From the school's point of view it can seem to be a lot of trouble and extra stress to admit as many as eight new children simultaneously with little notice. This can be especially so when their stay is likely to be short and at busy times of the year, such as Christmas or during national tests. It is also inevitable that schools take a long-term view of the majority of their work. However, many have recognised that having Traveller children in school has broadened everyone's experience and introduced new perspectives.

From the Traveller parents' point of view the question 'Is it worth it?' often refers to the length of time they will be allowed to stay at a stopping place and whether, in the circumstances, school will be feasible for their children. It hardly ever refers to education. Most Traveller parents want education for their children.

For the children themselves there are the difficulties of continually making new relationships and learning new rules and routines. However, given a positive welcome and enough support, most children demonstrate their enjoyment of school and their desire to learn.

The work of the Traveller Education Service has been organised to maximise continuity and ensure that each school's contribution is a valued part of an incremental process of learning for the children. Our experience has been that the schools have, to their great credit, endeavoured to do the most they can for the new children and given the children and Traveller Education Service staff a warm welcome. We think that the evidence demonstrates that it *is* worth it.

Drawing by John, age 7, March 1995

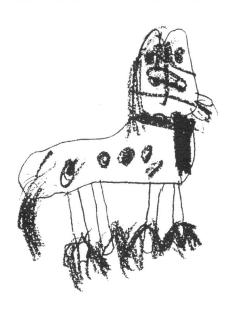

My Horses

I have got two horses, Peggy-Pony and Spot.
They are both in foal.
Spot is brown and white and Peggy-Pony is black and white.
Peggy-Pony is broken in for a cart, but she's too fat for the cart now.
The harness would be too tight.

by Joe

BIBLIOGRAPHY

Advisory Committee for the Education of Romany and other Travellers (ACERT) (ed.) (1993) *The Education of Gypsy and Traveller Children; Action Research and Coordination.* Hatfield, University of Hertfordshire Press.

Acton, Thomas and Kenrick Donald (1984) *Romani Rokkeripen To-Divvus.* London, Romanestan Publications.

Bearne Eve (ed) (1995) *Greater Expectations – Children reading Writing.* London, Cassell.

Department for Education (1994) *School Attendance Policy and Practice on Categorisation of Absence.* Crown Copyright.

Department for Education and Science (1985) *Education for All : the report of the Committee of Enquiry into the Education of Children from Ethnic Minority Groups.* London, HMSO.

Department for Education and Science and National Foundation for Education and Research (DES/NFER) (1989) *Partnership Teaching* London, HMSO.

Earle Fiona, Dearling Alan, Whittle Helen, Glasse Roddy and Gubby (1994) *A Time to Travel? An introduction to Britain's newer Travellers.* Dorset, Enabler Publications.

Essex County Council Education *Every Learner – A Framework for the Curriculum in Essex.* Essex County Council Education (1992).

European Federation for the Education of the Children of Occupational Travellers *What is your School doing for Travelling Children? A Guide to Equal Opportunities Through Distance Learning.* Efecot UK Steering Committee Coordinator c/o T.P. Riley School, Lichfield Road, Bloxwich, Walsall WS3 3LX.

Goodlad S. and Hirst B. (eds) (1990) *Explorations in Peer Tutoring.* Oxford, Blackwell Educational.

Hawes D. and Perez B. (1995) *The Gypsy and the State. The Ethnic Cleansing of British Society.* Bristol, School of Advanced Urban Studies (SAUS).

Kenny M. and O'Reilly M. (1996) *Black Stones round the Green Shamrock.* Dublin, Pavee Point.

McCann M., O'Siochain S. and Ruane J. (eds) (1994) *Irish Travellers, Culture and Ethnicity.* Institute of Irish Studies, The Queen's University, Belfast.

Microsoft *Encarta 96* CD-ROM.

Nursing Times volume 89. No. 33, 1993.

Ofsted (Office for Standards in Education) (1994) *Educational Support for Minority Ethnic Communities. A survey of educational provision funded under Section 11 of the 1966 Local Government Act.* Reference 130/94/NS.

Ofsted (Office for Standards in Education) (March 1996) *The Education of Travelling Children, A survey of educational provision for Travelling children.* Reference HMR/12/96/NS

O'Reilly, M. (1993) *With Travellers.* Dublin, Blackrock Teachers' Centre.

Rowe Don and Newton Jan (1994) *You, Me Us, Social and Moral Responsibility for Primary Schools.* Citizenship Foundation, sponsored by the Home Office. Reference CFPK1

Showman's Guild of Great Britain (1989) *Grand Centenary Fair 1889-1989 Souvenir Brochure.* The Showman's Guild of Great Britain, Central Office, Guild Hall, 41 Clarence Street, Staines, Middlesex TW18 4SY

Smith, Brigid (1994) *Through Writing to Reading.* Routledge.

West Midlands Education Service for Travelling Children, *Traveller Broadsheets.* (n.d.) Wolverhampton, WMESTC.

Legislation Section References

Brayne, Hugh and Martin, Gerry (1993) *Law for Social Workers.* London, Blackstone Press.

Clements, L. (1994) *Travellers' Rights.* Adviser, Number 46, November – December.

Clements, L. (1995) *Gypsy Policy after the Criminal Justice and Public Order Act 1994.* Paper to School of Advanced Urban Studies (SAUS), Gypsy Policy Seminar, Bristol, 21/2/1995.

Department of the Environment and the Welsh Office Circulars 18/94 and 76/94 *Gypsy Sites Policy and Unauthorised Camping.*

Hansard (HC) vol. 241, London, HMSO.

Hansard (HL) vol. 556, London, HMSO.

The Children's Society (1994) *Out of Site, Out of Mind.*

Advice on publications which show positive images of a travelling lifestyle, suitable for use with children, may be obtainable from a local Traveller Education Support Service.

Teachers in Essex can obtain information from:
The Traveller Education Service
The Traveller Education Centre
Alec Hunter High School
Stubbs Lane
Braintree
Essex CM7 3NT

NATT, The National Association for Teachers of Travellers c/o WMESTC, The Graisley Centre, Pool Street, Wolverhampton, WV2 2NE, should be able to advise of a local contact address elsewhere in the United Kingdom, if needed.